P9-BVM-744

0 00 30 0256845 3

1-00

No Longer the Property of
Hayner Public Library District

L.S.
027.6
POO

Poor people and
library services.

$26.50

DATE			

HAYNER PUBLIC LIBRARY DISTRICT
ALTON, ILLINOIS

OVERDUES .10 PER DAY. MAXIMUM FINE
COST OF BOOKS. LOST OR DAMAGED BOOKS
ADDITIONAL $5.00 SERVICE CHARGE.

BAKER & TAYLOR

POOR PEOPLE AND LIBRARY SERVICES

Edited by
Karen M. Venturella

FOREWORD BY
Sanford Berman

McFarland & Company, Inc., Publishers
Jefferson, North Carolina, and London

HAYNER PUBLIC LIBRARY DISTRICT
ALTON, ILLINOIS

British Library Cataloguing-in-Publication data are available

Library of Congress Cataloguing-in-Publication Data

Poor people and library services / edited by Karen M. Venturella ;
   foreword by Sanford Berman.
        p.   cm.
      Includes bibliographical references and index.
      ISBN 0-7864-0563-5 (sewn softcover : 50# alkaline paper)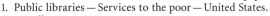
      1. Public libraries — Services to the poor — United States.
   I. Venturella, Karen M., 1962–   .
   Z711.92.P66P66   1998
   027.6 — dc21   98-21071
                                                              CIP

©1998 Karen M. Venturella. All rights reserved

*No part of this book may be reproduced or transmitted in any form
or by any means, electronic or mechanical, including photocopying
or recording, or by any information storage and retrieval system,
without permission in writing from the publisher.*

Manufactured in the United States of America

*McFarland & Company, Inc., Publishers
   Box 611, Jefferson, North Carolina 28640*

L.5.
027.6
02
p00

ADJ-6844

To my parents who taught me to
treat every person, rich or poor,
with dignity and integrity.

Table of Contents

ACCESS TO TECHNOLOGY
FOR LOW-INCOME GROUPS

NEIGHBORHOOD COALITION
AND INTERNATIONAL ORGANIZATION

SUGGESTIONS FOR ACTION

PROGRAMS IN SHELTERS AND PUBLIC HOUSING

RURAL POVERTY PROGRAMS

Acknowledgments

I would like to thank the contributors, most of whom I have spoken with on the telephone but never met. I hope our paths cross. Thank you for helping me to make this book a reality. It truly amazed me that I was able to phone people I had never met and get their commitment to writing a chapter for this book. There are many incredible people in this world who believe in what they do and who are willing to take the time to share their program ideas with others. I hope their devotion comes back to them a hundredfold and they are able to get glimpses of the positive effect they have on people's lives.

My dream is that a library school student may come across this book while engaging in that ancient habit of perusing the shelves. It is too much to hope that a bolt of lightning strike and their professional life is changed forever. But maybe it will stimulate some thoughts.

Karen Venturella
February 1998

ix

Foreword

BY SANFORD BERMAN

In June 1990, at its annual conference in Chicago, the American Library Association (ALA) membership, and then Council, approved a "Policy on Library Services to Poor People." Originally drafted by the Minnesota Library Association's Social Responsibilities Round Table (MSRRT), it had first been submitted to ALA's Social Responsibilities Round Table (SRRT), which passed it in January 1990. Subsequently, ALA's Executive Board charged another ALA unit, the Coordinating Committee on Access to Information (CCAI), with implementing the resolution. However, CCAI did not immediately and vigorously plunge into implementation, but rather decided to "reanalyze the policy through referral to affected units," one possible outcome being that CCAI would "recommend that Council rescind its former action and refer the resolution for study by affected units." Some of those units, CCAI noted, "may want to come back with recommenda-tion/revisions." On June 21, 1991, fully one year after passage, I wrote Arthur Curley, the CCAI chair:

> Dear Arthur:
>
> Maybe I'm Overreacting. Maybe. At any rate, someone just sent me your Atlanta agenda and attached documents. And while I'm fully prepared to believe that the Committee has acted out of "good intention," I am deeply disturbed about how CCAI has, in fact, handled the "Poor People's Policy."
>
> Being one of the principal drafters, I remind the Committee that the Policy was distributed to everyone attending last year's Member-ship Meeting. It was duly debated and approved, then forwarded to Council, which I understand accepted it, referring the document to

1

your committee for *implementation*, not *dismemberment* or *revision*. Further, the draft policy had been published in several journals beforehand and also sent — by me personally — to several ALA units, including the OLOS Advisory Committee and PLA, none of which responded with either criticism or suggestions. My (fairly obvious) point here is that this was hardly a secretive undertaking, we *did* solicit input beyond SRRT, and the ALA Membership *did* pass the policy as submitted.

Also worth stating (again) is that we modeled the document on the existing Minority Concerns Policy in the (perhaps naive) belief that doing so would enhance its acceptance and implementation (in terms of form, language, etc.). However, this policy — by definition — while it includes minorities (if poor), is by no means *limited* in scope to minorities. Low-income people may be white or of color.

I have no quarrel whatever with referring portions of the Membership/Council–approved policy to various units for recommendations on *how to implement it*. But I genuinely fear CCAI has betrayed the intention of Membership and Council alike by inviting *revisions*. I can say unequivocally that it has violated and distorted the intention of the policy originators.

Frankly, some of the mentioned "concerns" or "novelties" connected with the policy I do not comprehend. For instance, what's the "trouble" with paying stipends or providing transportation to members of low-income advisory boards? First, it's elementary common sense. If you really want such people to advise on policy and services, they must be able to attend meetings, etc. And second, the provision is not *law*, it's a guideline, a recommendation, a "permission" for individual libraries to do it. So what's up here? What's the conflict? What's the worry? Similarly, the encouragement of staff foodshelf donations and anti-hunger activity is exactly that: encouragement (not a "requirement"). Many libraries already conduct foodshelf donation drives among staff and canvas for United Way and other charitable groups. These are not utterly earthshaking ideas. But what's important is to declare them as *good and desirable*, as something the whole profession thinks should be done to address an absolutely critical and worsening problem.

And much of the now "Dismembered" policy is rooted solidly in the existing ALA canon, which — among other things — enjoins librarians to be proactive in fostering information access and to not charge fees.

Yours is the Access Committee. The simple truth is that poor people *do not enjoy the same access to library resources and information that people with adequate incomes do*. The basic cause, certainly, is poverty itself and a socioeconomic system that permits it. But that doesn't let librarians "off the hook." There are many things we can do to serve poor people directly and to direct public attention to the continuing problem of poverty and how it can be lessened, if not eradicated. It is a lie to talk about "free public libraries" and "equality of service" when large parts of the population can't afford to get to the library, can't afford video and other fees, can't afford fines, and are often so ill-housed and fed and without health insurance (which translates into substandard, if any, medical care) that they cannot even exploit or enjoy library resources that *are* available to the same (or comparable) extent as people who *do* have adequate housing, food, and health care. To me — and, I trust, to you, too— this is not just unacceptable: it's scandalous. And requires immediate attention and action, not bureaucratic game playing.

Though no one invited me, I'll try to attend the Committee meeting. But whether I do or not, I ask the Committee to firmly and quickly commit itself to making the Poor People's Policy a reality: a declaration to and by the profession that we will not tolerate destructive inequality based on how much money someone happens to have.

What happened afterwards? Nothing. The policy didn't get rescinded or "revised," but neither was it made real. Indeed, to this day (December 1996) it has never been fully published in ALA's official organ, *American Libraries.* It did, though, trigger a March 1991 *American Libraries* editorial by Leonard Kniffel that trashed the policy as "flabby-minded," "useless" and "absurd," in the process equating homeless people with Charles Manson. In reply, I sent this message to editor Tom Gaughan on March 3rd:

Dear Tom,

I honestly don't know how to say this nicely and "coolly." So maybe I should just say it directly, no matter how it comes out: Leonard Kniffel's "Ed. Notes" in the March 1991 issue I found almost literally painful and deeply disturbing. Let me state immediately that I do not contest Kniffel's right to express his views nor AL's to publish them. What troubles me? The monumental ignorance about who the poor, hungry, and homeless really are. (I was — with my family — once both homeless and on food stamps!) What I can only describe as cruel, if not vicious, stereotyping of poor and homeless people. And a serious misrepresentation of the "Poor People's Policy" passed last summer by ALA Membership, which few readers are likely to appreciate since no major library periodical has printed the full text.

Most outrageous and hurtful, of course, is the intentional equation of "Charles Manson" with poor and homeless people:

Poor person – Crazed, evil-smelling brute

That is at once pathetic and preposterous.

I trust that Kniffel's statement will generate suitable responses. But I truly believe that more is necessary. So I propose and urge that *American Libraries* publish — in the April issue if at all possible — the complete "Poor People's Policy," my testimony at the declarations by poor people and anti-poverty advocates themselves, and at least a few statistics to suggest the depth and breadth of poverty in this country. To simplify things, I'm enclosing the original policy as well as my hearing remarks and statistics.

Quote any of the above that you wish. My hope is that Kniffel's mean-minded and uninformed editorial may — at minimum — stimulate an overdue discussion on what poverty means to all of us and what role libraries should assume in ending it.

A few letters appeared in the May and June 1991 issues contesting Kniffel's classist remarks. And that's it. At least until 1996, when in the course of ALA's Midwinter conclave in San Antonio, I asked each of the three ALA presidential hopefuls if they would assign high priorities to implementing the long-dormant policy. All said they would. Later, in October, the president-elect, Barbara Ford, thanked me for responding to her questionnaire on "the developing presidential program for 1997–98." She asked: "What are the most important issues for ALA to address in the next two years?" My recommendation: "Issues of class and poverty as barriers to equal and effective library use." Her second question: "What would you suggest as presidential themes, initiatives, and programs that would benefit you and other members?" My answer:

- Immediate promotion and implementation of the "Poor People's Policy" adopted in 1990.
- Increased budgetary and staff support for OLOS (Office for Literacy and Outreach Services).

Said Ford: "As you know, I am interested in the "Poor People's Policy," which you listed as an initiative that would benefit you and other ALA members. What would you suggest to implement this policy?" I responded on October 28, 1996, with a laundry list:

- Publish the whole policy in *American Libraries*, perhaps with a few tips on local implementation from Sherry Lampman's enclosed list. (Lampman coordinated Tax Credit Awareness Campaigns for the Minnesota Alliance for Children from 1992 to 1995.)
- Designate OLOS as the ALA agency to coordinate and promote policy-implementation, making this mandate equal to OLOS'

responsibility regarding literacy and ensuring that there is adequate funding and staff to effectively address both mandates.

- Instruct ALA's Washington office to actively support legislative initiatives that would contribute to reducing, if not eliminating, poverty itself (e.g., a living minimum wage, adequate welfare payments, more low-income housing, and national health insurance, all cited in the "Poor People's Policy").
- Produce through ALA Publishing Services a policy-based leaflet or brochure, replete with resource and bibliographic citations.
- Urge, as President, that the Library of Congress undertake the cataloging reforms specified in the enclosed SRRT "Resolution on Subject Headings Related to Class and Poverty."
- Revive OLOS' newsletter *Empowerment* as a vehicle for antipoverty, proliteracy news, ideas, and networking data.
- Mount a major conference program on issues of class and poverty as serious barriers to equal and effective library use. Possible speakers: Marion Wright Edelman, Rep. Bernie Sanders (VT), Rep. Major Owens (NY), Rep. Martin Olav Sabo (MN), Sen. Paul Wellstone (MN), Mollie Ivins, Jim Hightower, Rep. Maxine Waters (CA).
- Request that all ALA units undertake poverty-related projects and programs.

So far (February 1998), still nothing. But we'll see.

While few Americans would have known it from the mainstream or library press (I found out in a Canadian antipoverty paper), the United Nations had declared 1996 to be the International Year for the Eradication of Poverty. Once I learned that, I sent a "Letter to the Editor" to both *American Libraries* and *Library Journal* (August 3 and September 24, respectively). To date, neither has been printed. So just for the record, here's the unpublished *LJ* missive:

> Dear Colleagues,
> I admire Charles Robinson's candor in declaring that he and his BCPL Deputy Director are "middle-class people serving the middle class" (Sept. 1, 1996, p. 138). Neither he nor Jean-Barry Molz would probably even know (much less care) that 1996 is the U.N.–declared International Year for the Eradication of Poverty. But the library press should know — and care, especially since working and poor people have just as much a right to library service as the middle and upper classes, not to mention an arguably greater need.
> To support and celebrate the International Year, *LJ* (and sister periodicals) could finally print in full ALA's policy on "Library Services to Poor People" adopted in 1990, perhaps with practical suggestions for implementing it. And it would also be helpful to

publish the recent Social Responsibilities Round Table–approved "Resolution on Subject Headings Related to Class and Poverty," which other individuals and groups may wish to endorse. Finally, colleagues who believe that libraries have both an obligation and opportunity to serve everyone in their communities, not just the comfortable and wealthy, can contact or join SRRT's Task Force on Hunger, Homelessness, and Poverty: c/o S. Berman, 4400 Morningside Road, Edina MN 55416.

Having alluded more than once to subject headings and cataloging, I am presenting on pages 6 to 13 a few documents and examples that attest to how inadequately libraries provide access to poverty-related resources — and also demonstrate how that sorry situation might be improved. First, this is the SRRT resolution (also a petition) to the Library of Congress that seeks to improve resource-access by changing several unhelpful headings (for instance, converting PUBLIC WELFARE to simply WELFARE) and finally establishing dozens of forms to represent real topics — like CLASSISM, CORPORATE WELFARE, and WORKING POOR PEOPLE — that so far have been unrecognized and thus rendered invisible and unreachable in library catalogs:

Resolution on Subject Headings Relating to Class and Poverty

Whereas the American Library Association in 1990 adopted a "Poor People's Services Policy" that promotes, in part, "the ready accessibility of print and nonprint materials that honestly address the issues of poverty and homelessness, that deal with poor people in a respectful way, and that are of practical use to low-income patrons"; and

Whereas that same policy encourages activities and programs "likely to reduce, it not eliminate, poverty itself"; and

Whereas Library of Congress subject headings can importantly affect access to vital library resources on hunger, homelessness, and poverty, as well as shaping library users' attitudes toward those topics; and

Whereas LC headings currently impede or distort access to much relevant material because of antiquated or insensitive language, coupled with a failure to recognize a host of significant subjects actually represented in library collections;

Therefore be it resolved that the 1,800-member Social Responsibilities Round Table of the American Library Association urges the Library of Congress to (a) replace PUBLIC WELFARE and PUBLIC WELFARE ADMINISTRATION with the more familiar forms WELFARE and WELFARE ADMINISTRATION; (b) humanize the current heading, POOR by transforming it into POOR PEOPLE; and (c) swiftly establish and assign these warranted and essential headings related to poverty, hunger, homelessness and social policy:

CHILD LABOR EXPLOITATION
CHILDREN OF UNEMPLOYED PARENTS
CLASSISM
CLASSISM IN CAPITAL PUNISHMENT
CLASSISM IN CHILDREN
CLASSISM IN ECONOMIC POLICY
CLASSISM IN EDUCATION
CLASSISM IN ENVIRONMENTAL POLICY
CLASSISM IN INTELLIGENCE TESTS
CLASSISM IN LAW
CLASSISM IN LIBRARIANSHIP
CLASSISM IN LITERATURE
CLASSISM IN MASS MEDIA
CLASSISM IN MEDICAL CARE
CLASSISM IN SOCIAL POLICY
CLASSISM IN TAXATION
CLASSISM IN TEXTBOOKS
CLASSISM IN THE CRIMINAL JUSTICE
   SYSTEM
CORPORATE POWER
CORPORATE WELFARE
DEMOCRATIC SOCIALISM
ECONOMIC DEMOCRACY
FOOD SHELVES
GRASSROOTS MOVEMENT
HOMELESS AFRO-AMERICAN WOMEN
HOMELESS BOYS
HOMELESS FAMILIES

HOMELESS FAMILY SERVICES
HOMELESS GIRLS
HOMELESS MENTALLY ILL PERSONS
HOMELESS MENTALLY ILL PERSONS'
   SERVICES
HOMELESS PEOPLE IN ART
HOMELESS PEOPLE'S ADVOCATES
HOMELESS PEOPLE'S ART
HOMELESS TEENAGERS
HOMELESSNESS—ACTION PROJECTS
HUNGER—ACTION PROJECTS
HUNGER ACTIVISTS
INTERCLASS FRIENDSHIP
LOW-INCOME HOUSING
MARXISM
NONCLASSIST CHILDREN'S LITERATURE
POOR AFRO-AMERICAN FAMILIES
POOR FAMILIES
POOR PARENTS
POOR PEOPLE—EMPOWERMENT
POOR PEOPLE—RIGHTS
POOR SINGLE MOTHERS
RIGHT TO SHELTER
VIOLENCE AGAINST HOMELESS PEOPLE
VIOLENCE AGAINST POOR PEOPLE
WELFARE CONSUMERS—RIGHTS
WORKING POOR PEOPLE

Copies to: Chief, Cataloging Policy & Support Office, Library of Congress, Washington, DC 20540; Library Press. Submitted by Sanford Berman, Coordinator, SRRT Task Force on Hunger, Homelessness and Poverty, July 6, 1996.

———————————————————

And these are actual cases of massive LC under-cataloging, together with examples of how Hennepin County Library (HCL) handled the same works:

LIBRARY OF CONGRESS CATALOGING-IN-PUBLICATION DATA
Sidel, Ruth.
Keeping women and children last : America's war on the poor / Ruth Sidel.
Sequel to: Women and children last.
Includes bibliographical references (p.   ) and index.
1. Poor women — United States.   2. Public welfare — United States.
3. Family policy — United States.   4. Women heads of households — United States.   I. Sidel, Ruth. Women and children last.   II. Title.

HCL Cataloging Record

100	Sidel, Ruth, $d 1933–
245	Keeping women and children last: $b America's war on the poor.
260	New York: $b Penguin Books, $c 1996.
500	Sequel to Women and children last.
505	PARTIAL CONTENTS: Assault on the female-headed family. -Who are the poor? -Targeting welfare recipients. -Teenagemothers: casualties of a limited future. -Poor children: the walking wounded.
650	Poor children $x Government policy
650	Poor families $x Government policy
650	Poor women $z United States $x Government policy.
650	Single teenage mothers $x Government policy.
650	Welfare reform
650	Women-headed families $x Government policy.
650	Classism in social policy
650	Sexism in social policy.
650	Ageism in social policy.
740	Women and children last.
740	America's war on the poor.
740	War on the poor.

LIBRARY OF CONGRESS CATALOGING-IN-PUBLICATION DATA
Merchants of misery :
how corporate America profits from poverty /
edited by Michael Hudson.
Includes index.
1. Financial services industry — United States.   2. Financial services industry — United States — Corrupt practices.   3. Poor — United States.
I. Hudson, Michael, 1961—

HCL Cataloging Record

100	Hudson, Michael, $d 1961-$eeditor.
245	Merchants of misery: $b how corporate America profits from poverty
260	Monroe, ME : $b Common Courage Press, $c copyright 1996.
505	PARTIAL CONTENTS: Preface, by Maxine Waters. -The geography of discrimination: banking, race and redlining. -Small loans, big profits: the finance company business. -The shadow banks: pawnshops and check cashers. -Mortgaging your future: home-loan rip-offs. -

505 Driven to debt: high-priced car loans and insurance. -No place like home: the business of slum lords. -A few bucks a week: the rent-to-own industry. -Schools for scandal: trade school scams. -The politics of rich and poor: the struggle over corporate profit and consumer rip-offs. PARTIAL APPENDICES: How to investigate businesses that profit from the poor. -Resources.
591 1996
650 Classism in business
650 Redlining.
650 Financial services industry $x Corrupt practices.
650 Pawnbrokers $x Corrupt practices.
650 Check cashing services $x Corrupt practices.
650 Real estate business $x Corrupt practices.
650 Mortgage fraud.
650 Money lenders $x Corrupt practices.
650 Slumlords.
650 Technical institutes $x Corrupt practices
650 Consumers $x Rights.
650 Discrimination in bank loans.
650 Exploitation $x Case studies.
650 Poor consumers $x Discrimination
650 Poor consumers $x Self-help materials
650 Mortgage brokers $x Corrupt practices
650 Automobile loan fraud
650 Rent-to-own stores $x Corrupt practices
700 Waters, Maxine
710 Common Courage Press.
740 Misery merchants.
740 How corporate America profits from poverty
740 Corporate America profits from poverty
740 Corporate poverty profits
740 Poverty profits

LIBRARY OF CONGRESS CATALOGING-IN-PUBLICATION DATA

Wolf, Bernard, date.
Homeless/written and photographed by Bernard Wolf.
    1. Homeless children — New York (N.Y.) — Juvenile literature.
2. Henry Street Settlement (New York, N.Y.) — Juvenile literature.
3. Shelters for the homeless — New York (N.Y.) — Juvenile literature.
[1. Homeless persons.   2. Poor — New York (N.Y.)   3. Family life — New York (N.Y.)]   I. Title.

HCL Cataloging Record

100	Wolf, Bernard, $d 1930–
245	Homeless. $c Written and photographed by Bernard Wolf.
260	New York : $b Orchard Books, $c copyright 1995.
520	Color photos and a first-person narrative tell the story of 8-year-old Mikey and his family, who get a temporary rent-free apartment and help in the search for permanent housing from the Henry Street Settlement Urban Family Center in New York City's Lower East Side. Includes material on public assistance and food stamps..
610	Henry Street Settlement Urban Family Center, New York City.
650	Homeless children $z Lower East Side, New York City $x Personal narratives.
650	Homeless families $z Lower East Side, New York City.
650	Homeless people's shelters $z Lower East Side, New York City.
650	Eight-year-old boys $z Lower East Side, New York City
650	Welfare consumers $z Lower East Side, New York City
650	Food stamp consumers $z Lower East Side, New York City
650	Homeless families $x Pictorial works
650	Homeless children $x Pictorial works
650	Homeless people's shelters $x Pictorial works
651	Lower East Side, New York City $x Social conditions.

Library of Congress Cataloging-in-Publication Data

Confronting poverty : prescriptions for change / edited by Sheldon H.
Danziger, Gary D. Sandefur, and Daniel H. Weinberg.
    "The chapters in this volume were initially presented at a conference
held in May 1992 in Madison, Wisconsin, jointly sponsored by the
Institute for Research on Poverty at the University of Wisconsin-Madison
and the Office of the Assistant Secretary for Planning and Evaluation in
the U.S. Department of Health and Human Services"— Pref.
    Includes bibliographical references and index.
    1. Poverty — United States — Congresses.   2. Public welfare —
United States — Congresses.   3. United States — Social policy —
Congresses.   I. Danziger, Sheldon.   II. Sandefur, Gary D., 1951–
III. Weinberg, Daniel H.

HCL Cataloging Record

100	Danziger, Sheldon H.
245	Confronting poverty : $b prescriptions for change. $c Edited by Sheldon H. Danziger, Gary D. Sandefur, and Daniel H. Weinberg.

260 Cambridge, MA : $b Harvard University Press, $c copyright 1994.

500 "A Russell Sage Foundation Book."

500 "The chapters in this volume were initially presented at a conference held in May 1992 in Madison, Wisconsin, jointly sponsored by the Institute for Research on Poverty at the University of Wisconsin-Madison and the Office of the Assistant Secretary for Planning and Evaluation in the U.S. Department of Health and Human Services."

505 PARTIAL CONTENTS: Historical record: trends in family income, in equality, and poverty. -Public spending on the poor: historical trends and economic limits. -Dynamics and intergenerational transmission of poverty and welfare participation. Underclass: concept, controversy, and evidence. -Single-mother families, economic insecurity, and government policy. -Updating urban policy. -Reform of health care for the nonelderly poor. -Systemic educational reform and social mobility: the school choice controversy. -Poverty and immigration in policy perspective. -Antipoverty policy, affirmative action, and racial attitudes. -Nature, causes, and cures of poverty: accomplishments from three decades of poverty research and policy.

650 Antipoverty programs $z United States.

650 Educational reform $x Economic aspects.

650 Immigration policy $x Economic aspects.

650 Medical care reform $x Economic effects.

650 Poverty $z United States.

650 Single parent family $x Government policy.

650 Underclass $z United States.

650 Unemployment $z United States $x Government policy

650 Urgan policy $x Economic aspects.

650 Welfare $z United States.

650 Human resources policy

650 Poverty $x Research

700 Sandefur, Gary, $d 1951-

700 Weinberg, Daniel H.

710 Russell Sage Foundation.

710 United States. $b Dept. of Health and Human Services $b Office of the Assistant Secretary for Planning and Evaluation.

710 University of Wisconsin, Madison. $b Institute for Research on Poverty.

LIBRARY OF CONGRESS CATALOGING-IN-PUBLICATION DATA

Garr, Robin.

Reinvesting in America : the grassroots movements that are feeding

the hungry, housing the homeless, and putting Americans back to work
/ Robin Garr.
   Includes index.
   ISBN 0-201-40756-6
   1. Charities — United States.   2. Voluntarism — United States.
3. Nonprofit organizations — United States.   I. Title.

HCL CATALOGING RECORD

100   Garr, Robin.
245   Reinvesting in America : $b the grassroots movements that are
        feeding the hungry, housing the homeless, and putting
        Americans back to work. $c Foreword by David Osborne.
260   Reading, Mass. : $b Addison-Wesley, $c copyright 1995.
500   Includes appendix listing "more than 180 grassroots initiatives in
        every state and the District of Columbia."
505   PARTIAL CONTENTS: People need food. -People need shelter.
        -People need decent housing. -People need education. -People
        need healthy children and families. -People need political power.
        -People need job skills. -People need work. -Lessons for all
        Americans.
591   1995
650   Social action.
650   Grassroots movement.
650   Grassroots movement $x Directories.
650   Hunger $x Action projects.
650   Homelessness $x Action projects.
650   Homeless people's shelters.
650   Employment programs.
650   Community education.
650   Antipoverty programs.
650   Poor people's services.
650   Low-income housing $x Action projects
650   Community development $x Action projects
650   Poor people $x Empowerment
700   Osborne, David.
740   Investing in America.
740   Grassroots movements that are feeding the hungry, housing the
        homeless, and putting Americans back to work.

LIBRARY OF CONGRESS CATALOGING-IN-PUBLICATION DATA

Gans, Herbert J.
   The war against the poor: the underclass and antipoverty policy /
Herbert J. Gans.

Includes bibliographical references and index.
1. Poor — United States. 2. Public welfare — United States.
3. Economic assistance, Domestic United States. I. Title

HCL CATALOGING RECORD

100	Gans, Herbert J., $d 1927-
245	The war against the poor: $b the underclass and antipoverty policy
260	New York : $b Basicbooks, $c copyright 1995.
505	PARTIAL CONTENTS: Labeling the poor. -The invention of the under-class label. -Policies against poverty and underservingness. -Joblessness and antipoverty policy in the twenty-first century.
650	Poverty $x Government policy.
650	Underclass $z United States.
650	Poor people $x Legal status, laws, etc.
650	Unemployment $x Government policy.
650	Antipoverty programs $z United States.
650	Poor people $z United States.
650	Stigma (Social psychology) $x Case studies.
650	Underclass (Word)
650	Classism $z United States.
650	Human resources policy
740	The underclass and antipoverty policy.
740	Antipoverty policy and the underclass.

It may sound like an unduly harsh judgment, but classism and elitism truly pervade the library profession. I've already furnished illustrations at the national level. Unfortunately, there's plenty of evidence locally, too, where most of us live and work. At one Midwestern public library, Chamber of Commerce bulletins and publications from a right-wing think tank are routinely circulated among managers, the Administration adamantly refusing to acknowledge that these materials are clearly biased toward property, wealth, and power and at minimum should be complemented by newsletters and reports from labor, consumer, and antipoverty sources. At another institution, the first proposal to emerge from a Revenue Generation Team — expected to produce some $100,000 yearly — was to double the fine rate on juvenile materials.

The Minnesota Library Association, which in 1990 adopted a Poor People's Policy identical to ALA's, afterward declined to include as legislative platform planks such MSSRT recommendations, all explicitly mandated by the 1990 policy, as "Support for fair and affordable housing, especially in suburban areas," "Support for single-payer health insurance system," "Support for extended transitional housing for homeless people," and opposition to "'Workfare,' 'Learnfare,' and similar 'welfare reform' proposals unless endorsed by poor people and welfare recipients groups like Up and Out of Poverty Now — St. Paul Women, Work, & Welfare." In effect, MLA arbitrarily nullified whole portions of its own policy. (A year or two earlier, the organization decided not to support a higher minimum wage — also specified in the policy — in large part because such a hike might adversely impact some low-wage Minnesota libraries!)

Well, for librarians and citizens committed to social justice and a genuinely fair "playing field," there's much to do, and this "cookbook" or "toolkit" should make the job easier.

THEORY AND BACKGROUND

History and Theory
of Information Poverty

BY JOHN BUSCHMAN

We have a bedrock of professional policy and principle which guides us — indeed instructs us — to make our services and collections accessible, equitably distributed, and responsive to the needs of "all the people of the community" as the Library Bill of Rights puts it.[1]* American Library Association policy is quite blunt: "all individuals [should] have equal access to libraries and information services." Specifically, there is policy which calls for "libraries [to] recognize their role in enabling poor people to participate fully in a democratic society" through policy objectives such as informational publications, information and referral, "equity in funding adequate library services for poor people" and "the removal of all barriers to library and information services, particularly fees" which are elsewhere described as "discriminatory"[2] (ALA Handbook 136, 146, 156-157). This is by no means the whole of ALA policy on the matter. There are other policies addressing equity of access to libraries, and the policies quoted here are quite long and specific on details. There is very little room to finesse or slip away from the responsibility we have assigned ourselves as a profession.

My thesis is that the historical connection between librarianship (the professionals and their institutions) and the poor is in the process of a fundamental change, driven by what has been called the "new public philosophy."[3] I do not consider this change to be for the better, nor do I consider the process to be irreversible. I do not contend that there is no significant and valuable work for and with the poor happening in librarianship right now.

*See Notes at the end of the chapter.

As an institution, we are not separate from the dominant trends of our market-driven culture and a new vision of the role of public institutions. However, I think it is important to understand this in some historical perspective. This chapter, first, briefly outlines and characterizes the historical purpose and role of American libraries in service to the poor up to the 1980s. This is followed by a review of what scholars like Sheldon Wolin (1981)[4] and Henry Giroux (1987)[5] have called the "new public philosophy" and its contrasting values for public institutions like schools and libraries. The next section focuses on how librarianship has adapted and reacted to the "new public philosophy" and the consequences to our professional services — and our professional values — concerning serving the poor. There is a specific focus on the issues of fees and access to new electronic resources.

American Library Service to the Poor—An Overview

The definition of the "poor" in relationship to libraries has been historically flexible and contingent upon conditions and social attitudes of the time. Therefore, we should not be guilty of reading backwards too strictly as to who were the "poor" to be served by libraries.

Let us begin by looking past the social and early circulating library movement in colonial and post-colonial America since both essentially relied upon a membership who could afford to pay for the privilege.[6] It was in the nineteenth century that the great era of public institution-building took place. As numerous authors note, the development of free public schooling went hand-in-hand with the development of the free public library (Harris 1976, Gates, Wiegand, Ditzion).[7] Indeed, George Ticknor's plans for the Boston Public Library were pitched as the "crowning glory of the school system."[8] Both institutions shared the institutional quest for universal literacy with the idea that, as was stated at the time, the "intellectual and literary common" would be available to "the rich and poor ... the high and lowly born, the masses who wield the hammers...."[9] Michael Harris called this vision of their founding the "liberal and idealistic commitment to the public library as a 'people's university'."[10] The poor were then defined as those who did manual labor, who could not afford to own the library or private tutoring of the wealthy. Very often there was a certain relentlessness about library programs to uplift the poor. As Sidney Ditzion put it, "The poor, whom the Lord loved so well as to make them numerous, were a matter of first concern to the public library interests. No extended argument was necessary to carry the conviction that those who were in straitened means by accident of birth, or otherwise through no fault of their own, were deserving of the educational and inspirational influences of books."[11]

This version of American library history was a long-held myth. Behind that myth there was a substantial measure of social control exercised under the assumption that "good reading led to good social behavior; bad reading ... inevitably led to bad social behavior.... [L]ibrarians' attitudes toward censorship were generally ambivalent, sometimes openly supportive" and they viewed their responsibility as a "duty to protect local communities from the assumed effects of 'bad' reading" and to select books for their "prudent counsel and guidance ... and naturally they wanted all classes to society to benefit from exposure to them."[12] Revisionist interpretations have been quite critical of the leaders of the era. Specifically, those who founded public libraries were quite explicit in their desire to assimilate the influx of immigrants, whom George Ticknor felt "at no time consisted of persons who ... were fitted to understand our free institutions or to be entrusted with the political power given by universal suffrage."[13] Even the traditional Horatio Alger stories of self improvement among the "respectable poor" were supported with the argument that such persons "tended to increase the productivity and wealth of the community."[14] The public library was something of an elitist, authoritarian institution designed to support both the education of a new elite, and "to educate people so that they might follow the best men and not demagogues [and] to stabilize the republic" in a time of heavy immigration.[15]

Revisionist history notwithstanding, the essential "democratic dogma" (as it has been called) of the public library as an instrument of universal public enlightenment was well-supported by the public with its tax dollars (if not heavy use by either the middle classes or the poor) for well over 120 years. It was only questioned once the bedrock article of faith — education "as the key ingredient in America's particular recipe for progress and prosperity" — began to be questioned about twenty years ago.[16] Therefore it is historically accurate to characterize libraries as public institutions founded upon a long-held public consensus — however authoritarian — to equalize educational and self-improvement opportunity for the working poor.

The Era of Intellectual Freedom

The next broadly defined era in librarianship was the development of intellectual freedom as a priority. Wayne Wiegand notes that the public widely resisted librarians' self-defined role as guardians against "bad" reading, and the benefits of censorship appeared less apparent with the book burning in Germany in the 1930s. He further notes that this movement culminated in the adoption of the Library Bill of Rights in 1939 by the American Library Association.[17] Others cite the rise in prominence of the ALA during this time, and trace other policies adopted by the Association which flowed from that initial 1939 statement of professional principles: the School Library Bill of Rights; the Statement on Professional Ethics; the Freedom to Read; and the ALA Statement on Labeling.[18] Michael Harris called this a "new philosophy of public library service in America," and there was a new emphasis on "the importance of the library's role as a guardian of the people's right to know…. This was to be done by giving all the people Bill free and convenient access to the nation's cultural heritage and the day's social intelligence."[19] Harris has further linked this period of library history to what he has termed a dominant pluralist perspective in librarianship. He outlined this perspective in detail, but of particular note here, he states that this ethos operates on the assumption that "all Americans are free to think as they choose" and that "librarians are committed to the First Amendment … and the Library Bill of Rights, and [they] maintain that commitment by remaining neutral relative to the contents and services of their libraries."[20]

The inherent problems with these assumptions are thoroughly dissected by Harris, but in sum, he concludes that "the pluralist perspective so widely and uncritically adopted by librarians has dictated long and broad structured silences relative to the ways in which social, economic, and cultural power relations shape the nature and extent of library service."[21] I agree, but would also argue that the inherent logic of such fundamental positions as the Library Bill of Rights led to its extension in later policies noted in the introduction to this paper. These policies go to lengths to stress equality of opportunity to level the informational playing field and thus act on the spirit of the initial principles of the Library of Rights. The argument that pure political equality meant very little in America without some measure of economic equality became common, and it found its way into librarianship in the form of those policies which strove to achieve an extended — and more radical — vision of neutrality. Advocates for library services to the poor put it quite plainly:

> In today's world, information is power. [AFDC] recipients struggle with information bureaucracies … constantly and we are aware of how our power as citizens is limited by our lack of information. As the numbers of poor women and children grow in this country, as [governments] continue to be unresponsive to the[ir] needs…, as low-income people become increasingly disenfranchised through a rise in illiteracy and a fall in educational opportunity, the role of the public library in providing information for citizenship for

low-income people is crucial. We need accessible public libraries and "accessible" means free of fines, fees and other structural barriers.[22]

What did this mean for library services to the poor during the period of roughly the 1930s to the 1980s? Essentially it meant the development of programs to address outreach in the form of bookmobiles, popular neighborhood locations, "community walks," information and referral services, and literacy programs. These are more or less the standard set of approaches we are familiar with which give "meaning to equal opportunity" in both the political and economic spheres.[23] There were, however, more progressive approaches in the 1960s and early 1970s, like Hardy Franklin's prescient paper to the ALA Conference arguing that librarians needed to take the lead in resisting the cutbacks in hours of branch libraries. "The public library," he argued, "must commit itself to the promotion of social progress and a better standard of life for all the people, but most especially, the poor."[24] Other approaches were less fundamental: taking books to the beach, a film -with-books series in a housing project; using rock and roll music, card tricks, and a decorated bookmobile to attract interest in reading; chartering buses to the library; training in work habits[25] and the use of a circulating toy library to enhance early literacy development[26] and parent-child relationships[27] were some of them. Such approaches probably contributed to the famous critiques of social responsibility in librarianship which charge that librarians were seeking "to resolve hundreds of ... social, scientific, or political issues, regardless of how vital they may be for the future of humanity."[28]

In sum, I agree with the analysis that this historical era began with the adoption of the Library Bill of Rights and would add that it was logically extended in policies and positions of the ALA which articulated yet further the notion of equal access and equal opportunity. These in turn fueled some novel and progressive extensions of library services in the 1960s and 1970s, and some critiques when public money began to tighten thereafter. I do not want to leave this section without noting, as before, that this work — and the professional ethics which drive it — continues still. Even while more wealthy suburban public libraries adopt stances hostile to the homeless, some city libraries are becoming more welcoming and proactive.[29] And as always, the Minnesota Social Responsibilities Round Table is there to draft policy calling for the "direct representation of poor people" and for putting "low-income programs and services into regular library budgets."[30] In all of this, the definition of the poor has become more contemporary: the economically disadvantaged — among whom minorities, women, and children are disproportionately represented — the homeless, and displaced workers have become the focus of library services for the poor.

The Era of the New Public Philosophy

We are now in what the scholar Sheldon Wolin has labeled as a new era which began with the election of Ronald Reagan as president:

> The importance of economics in public councils is not a Reagan innovation....
> It is rather that the prominence of economics is both the herald and the agent
> of a profound transformation in American political culture..... Economics
> thus becomes the paradigm of what public reason should be. It prescribes the
> form that "problems" have to be given before they can be acted upon, the
> kinds of "choices" that exist, and the meaning of "rationality".... When the
> economy becomes the polity, citizen and community become subversive words
> in the vocabulary of the new political philosophy.[31]

Communications scholars have noted particular (and by now familiar) trends in terms of information resources:

> Privatization ... involves moving the production and provision of commu-
> nications and information services from the public sector to the market, both
> by transferring ownership of key facilities to private investors and by mak-
> ing success in the marketplace the major criterion for judging the perfor-
> mance of all communications and information organizations (including those
> that remain in the public sector). This ... is accompanied by a parallel restruc-
> turing of consumption.... [T]he new market-oriented system of provision
> addresses people predominantly through their identity as consumers, both of
> the communications and information products they buy and of the products
> promoted in the expanding advertising system that finances many of the new
> services. In the process, the system marginalizes or displaces other identities,
> in particular the identity of citizen.[32]

In the words of Jacques Ellul, "the plurality of information does not help close the inequality."[33] There are now scholars of librarianship and communications who directly address and critique the fallout from the new public philosophy in our field.[34]

Librarianship and the Poor Under the New Public Philosophy

There are general trends in librarianship which indicate that the profession is and has been moving to align itself with the new public philosophy. For instance, the tremendous controversies and subsequent backlash over "social" or "nonlibrary" issues, which culminated in the Association of College and Research Libraries Board passing a policy to limit involvement in social issues and in actions within ALA to limit discussions raised by the Social Responsibilities Round Table.[35] There has further been a general blurring of roles between libraries and for-profit businesses, with libraries eagerly adapting for-profit goals and tactics.[36] An examination of how librarianship has handled the issues of fees and access to new electronic resources gives some specific detail to this analysis.

Fees for Services

The recent historical reasons for implementing fees are clear. As Leah Lievrouw puts it, "mass media systems are technologically complex and are expensive to develop [and] owners and operators have borne most of the costs of these systems." However, there is a cost-shifting to users in these new systems: "while some ... have advertising revenue, most information services depend on user fees for their income."[37] As librarianship has gravitated toward the new communication systems, this is precisely the choice and debate which has occurred. The initial flashpoint was the privatization of government information. As William noted, "When the government creates information, it has a duty to make that information available to citizens ... at the lowest possible cost or even on a subsidized basis.... We have seen a serious eroding of that principle.... [We now have a] cost-benefit analysis of government information activities, maximum reliance on the private sector, and cost recovery through user charges."[38] This is a direct contrast to the long standing tradition, in the words of a 1787 Federal Convention delegate, that "The people have the right to know what their Agents are doing or have done..."[39] and the "civic role of libraries" posits that public information underwrites effective public policy, democratic participation, and equity.[40]

The Reagan privatization of public information era was a harbinger of culture change in librarianship. Essentially, librarians were introduced to the notion that they were sitting on a form of "wealth" we were not fully exploiting. From this has grown the concept of "entrepreneurial" librarianship when librarians expect their resources (especially the electronic ones) to "produce income, or create a more favorable budgeting and fundraising environment." The range of such strategies has been considerable. From business fee-for-information centers to proposed cost-sharing for national cataloging data, this ethic is now a part of the landscape of librarianship.[41]

Herbert Schiller has called this state of affairs "an undemocratic information system," and he further notes that "it is no overstatement to argue that the survival of American librarianship and its principles, as they have been understood historically, are at stake."[42] It was in this context that the National Commission on Libraries and Information Science (NCLIS) completed a study in 1985 on "The Role of Fees in Supporting Library and Information Services in Public and Academic Libraries."[43] This landmark document maps out most if not all of the subsequent arguments for and against fees in the library literature, and situates the issue historically. It is therefore worth examining closely.

First, the report is an almost textbook breakdown of how public institutions like libraries have justified the charging of fees. For instance it was noted that "the 1980s are a period of dramatic change in how public institutions raise and invest financial resources.... In response to ... financial pressure, there has been a significant growth in the use of fees within the public sector..." citing its application in public utilities, recreation services and facilities, public transit, and elsewhere.[44] The telling detail is that, while the report sought to make "an objective statement of the complex issues related to the charging of fees [and] of the pro-fee and anti-fee arguments,"[45] its rhetorical weight leans toward a modification of the traditional no-fee ethic. Only roughly about 10 percent of the report effectively explores the non-fee issues; the rest focuses on implementation, softening the blow of fees, and the philosophical justification for fees.

In a classic example of the new public philosophy at work, the report noted that "the definition of a given service as a public good ... or a private good depends on the library's operating environment and perceptions of its role in the marketplace."[46] There never was a direct answer to the tradition of free library service or the discriminatory nature of fees. In fact, the report led off with the recommendations of the National Commission's Task Force on Library and Information Services to Cultural Minorities that the "benefit of the new technologies in libraries must be distributed equitably [and that] libraries should remove barriers [and] avoid charging fees that might create barriers...."[47] Instead, these were contrasted with the mom-and-apple-pie new public philosophy issues of a higher value and more recognition of libraries, efficiency, and basing services on need and demand.

What I see in all of this is the library version of a new public philosophy search for a justification to back away from national policies which have been consistently articulated as providing equity of access to information, which directly benefit primarily the poor. We are "exploring" and "clarifying" an issue which has been resolved for some time now. I would argue that the issue of charging fees (and fines as Sanford Berman notes) goes to the heart of library service to the poor. I would further argue that there is no such thing as a "value-added" library service which justifies a fee. If the service or collection provided falls within the mission of a library, then it should be offered like all other services or collections. There is no way to finesse the issue: Charging patrons for services discriminates against those who cannot pay.

Library Issues

There are a host of signs that would seem to indicate that equity of access is not being built into plans for new electronic networks and resources, nationally or in libraries. A major sign was the privatization of National Research and Education Network. The emphasis has been put on access for "problems in science and engineering with broad importance in economics and research."[48] Library applications were acknowledged as having a lower priority. Lago described the privatization framework adopted by Congress as leaving public institutions in a tenuous "third sector ... on the dole [and] in an atomized all-against-all beggars market."[49] Librarianship's response has been to try and carve out our niche or share of this "information market."

There is a wide acknowledgment that library access to electronic resources is clearly divided along economic lines. For instance, grant money for technology tends to flow to libraries already wealthy enough to have started purchasing technology, thus "replicat[ing] the pattern of computer resources benefiting those who already have socio-economic power."[50] Even in higher education, "historically black colleges, institutions serving American Indians, and those with large low-income populations" get the benefits of technology last.[51] Finally, one of the few national studies of access to computers among school children found "the predictable two-tier pattern" divided along racial and ethnic lines.[52]

When the issue of electronic resources is discussed in the library literature, copyright seems to come to the fore quite often. I am not advocating a radical rethinking of the concept of intellectual copyright. However, I do believe there is a tension between, first, our seeming consensus to uphold copyright for intellectual property owners and, second, our commitment to equity of service and access for the poor. I question Scott Bennett's bromide that "the public interest will flourish [and] computer technology is equally capable of advancing the goals of copyright owners *and* users."[53] His prescription for librarians to know and utilize the fair use doctrine is interesting, but ignores much of the context of the development of information systems. Generally, I have found that the enthusiasm for information technology has outweighed considerations of its negative impact. In this case, I think librarianship's focus on intellectual property rights has an unspoken primacy over equity of electronic access in our professional debates, and such priorities leave behind access for these resources for the poor.

As a solution to the continuing questions about funding public institutions, "many libraries are now learning to solicit funding based on their ability to advance their *communities'* objectives. An increasing number of communities are looking to networked technology to help develop their economies and to make their businesses more productive."[54] Again, I would argue that this is the voice of librarianship accommodating the new public philosophy of economic instrumentality for our institutions. In the process, we are not overtly repudiating service to the poor, but rather lowering its priority.

Perhaps the most pernicious effect is that librarians see the "adjustment" of their profession to this new environment as healthy and necessary. This goes beyond the crude introduction of profit-making strategies. Rather, those who seek to preserve the public mission of libraries make crucial concessions to the new public philosophy:

> Librarians have the opportunity to develop new roles within the rush of creativity that is being unleashed by networks. The opportunity, however, requires librarians to move beyond the questions of free or fee, just as the developing information infrastructure requires that we move beyond doubts about commercialization and public support.
>
> We also need to recognize that those ... who argue for the right to, or even the necessity of, charging fees for services, do so from a position of logic that is just as viable and defensible as those who passionately argue for maintenance of the public-good nature of free, subsidized service.[55]

This kind of approach simply reprioritizes our professional values without a debate. It is a well-intentioned argument to abandon much of our social responsibility — especially service to the poor — in favor of an easier path. In both this case and the one just noted, information technology (and, inherently, differing levels of access to it) is both the motivation and pretext for such changes. Librarianship has sought ways to pay for the capital investments in machinery, and to capitalize on its public appeal to make our institutions seem more vital. In the process, electronic access and services for the poor are an orphaned professional issue.

Conclusion

I believe there is serious cause for worry in librarianship about our commitment and ability to serve the poor. It is clear that the historical and economic basis of professional values which has guided an increasing commitment to equity of access is being eroded in the era of the new public philosophy. Our professional response seems to be that we must accommodate it to survive. We can see this new philosophy at work in librarianship's internal debates over fees and access to electronic services. What is most disturbing is the steady erosion of principle which drives our commitment to service. I believe strongly we need to follow Nancy Kranich's advice when she writes: "We must stand up and voice our legitimate concerns.... We must convince other stakeholders that they stand to gain from involving a vibrant civic sector in the new information marketplace. And, finally, we must revise the terms of the discourse. We must rekindle the concept of the informed citizenry. If we do not, no one else will."[56] I think it is fair to say that this is a more inspired vision of our profession than carving out a market niche.

Notes

1. Jean Key Gates, *Introduction to Librarianship*, 2d ed.(New York: McGraw-Hill, 1976): 255.

2. American Library Association, *ALA Handbook of Organization 1991/1992.* (Chicago: American Library Association, 1991): 136, 146, 157.

3. Henry A. Giroux, "Public Philosophy and the Crisis in Education," *Harvard Educational Review* 54,2 (1984): 186–194.

4. Sheldon Wolin, "The New Public Philosophy," *Democracy* 1,4 (1981): 23–36.

5. Henry A. Giroux, "Citizenship, Public Philosophy and the Struggle for Democracy," *Educational Theory.* 37,2 (1987): 103–119.

6. Jean Key Gates, *Introduction to Librarianship*, 2d ed. (New York: McGraw-Hill, 1976).

7. Ibid. / Michael H. Harris, "Public Libraries and the Decline of the Democratic Dogma," *Library Journal* (1 Nov. 1976): 2225–30. / Wayne A. Wiegand, "The Role of the Library in American History," *The Bowker Annual*, 33d ed. (New York: Bowker, 1988). / Sidney Ditzion, *Arsenals of a Democratic Culture* (Chicago: American Library Association, 1947).

8. Michael H. Harris, "The Purpose of the American Public Library," *Library Journal* 98 (15 Sept. 1973): 2509–14.

9. Sidney Ditzion, *Arsenals of a Democratic Culture* (Chicago: American Library Association, 1947): 22.

10. Michael H. Harris, "The Purpose of the American Public Library," *Library Journal* 98 (15 Sept. 1973): 2509.

11. Sidney Ditzion, *Arsenals of a Democratic Culture* (Chicago: American Library Association, 1947): 99.

12. Wayne A. Wiegand, "The Role of the Library in American History," *The Bowker Annual*, 33d ed. (NY: Bowker, 1988) 72-73.

13. Michael H. Harris, "The Purpose of the American Public Library," *Library Journal* 15 (15 Sept. 1973): 2510.

14. Edward C. Banfield, "Needed: A Public Purpose," *The Public Library and the City* , ed. Ralph W. Conant (Cambridge MA: MIT Press, 1965).

15. Michael H. Harris, "Public Libraries and the Decline of the Democratic Dogma," *Library Journal* 101 (1 Nov. 1976): 2226.

16. Ibid.

17. Wayne A. Wiegand, "The Role of the Library in American History," *The Bowker Annual*, 33d ed. (New York: Bowker, 1988): 72–73.

18. Jean Key Gates, *Introduction to Librarianship*, 2d ed. (New York: McGraw-Hill, 1976): 82.

19. Michael H. Harris, "The Purpose of the American Public Library," *Library Journal* 98 (15 Sept. 1973): 2514.

20. Michael H. Harris, "State, Class, and Cultural Reproduction: Toward a Theory of Library Service in the United States," *Advances in Librarianship* 14 (1986): 215.

21. *Ibid.*, 221.

22. William P. Davi, John Swan, and Sanford Berman, "Three Statements on Fees," in *Alternative Library Literature 1990/1991*, ed. James Danky and Sanford Berman (Jefferson NC: McFarland, 1992): 129.

23. Whitney North Seymour, Jr., and Elizabeth N. Layne, *For the People: Fighting for Public Libraries* (New York: Doubleday, 1970).

24. Hardy Franklin, *Keeping Libraries Open*, paper presented at the 95th ALA Annual Conference (Chicago, July 18–24, 1976) ED127 996, microfiche.

25. Eleanor Frances Brown, *Library Service to the Disadvantaged* (Metuchen NJ: Scarecrow 1971): 111–136.

26. Edythe O. Cawthorne, "Toys and Games—"The First Reading Tool," *School Library Journal* 21 (1975): 24–27.

27. Anne H. Rosenfeld, *Cultural Enrichment by Means of a Toy Library*, Parent-Child Program Series, Report No. 2 (National Institute of Mental Health, 1978) ED 175 185

28. David Berninghausen, "Antithesis in Librarianship: Social Responsibility vs. The Library Bill of Rights," *Library Journal* 97 (15 Nov. 1972): 3675.

29. Karen M. Venturella, "The Homeless and the Public Library," *Progressive Librarian* 3 (Summer 1991): 31–41.

30. Minnesota Social Responsibilities Round Table, "Poor People's Services," *Progressive Librarian* Preview edition (Summer 1990): 36–37.

31. Sheldon Wolin, "The New Public Philosophy," *Democracy* 1,4 (1981): 27–28, 36.

32. Graham Murdoch and Peter Golding, "Information Poverty and Political Inequality: Citizenship in the Age of Privatized Communication," *Journal of Communication* 39,3 (1989): 180.

33. Jacques Ellul, "Preconceived Ideas About Mediated Information," in *The Media Revolution in America and Western Europe* , ed. Everet M. Rogers & Francis Balle (Norwood NJ: Ablex, 1985): 106.

34. Henry T. Blanke, "Libraries and the Commercialization of Information," *Progressive Librarian* 2 (Winter 1990/1991): 9–13. / John Buschman, ed., *Critical Approaches to Information Technology in Librarianship* (Westport CT: Greenwood, 1993). / Herbert I. Schiller, The Global Commercialization of Culture," *Progressive Librarian* 2 (Winter 1990/1991): 15–22.

35. John Buschman, Mark Rosenzweig and Elaine Harger, "The Clear Imperative for Involvement: Librarians Must Address Social Issues," *American Libraries* (June 1994): 575–576.

36. John Buschman, ed., *Critical Approaches to Information Technology in Librarianship* (Westport CT: Greenwood, 1993): 215–216.

37. Leah Lievrouw, "Information Resources and Democracy: Understanding the Paradox," *Journal of the American Society for Information Science* 45,6 (1994): 353.

38. John Buschman,ed., *Critical Approaches to Information Technology in Librarianship* (Westport CT: Greenwood, 1993): 151–172.

39. Harold C. Relyea, "Dissemination of Government Information," *The Bowker Annual*, 41st ed., ed. Dave Bogart (New Providence NJ: Bowker, 1996): 221.

40. John Buschman, ed., *Critical Approaches to Information Technology in Librarianship* (Westport CT: Greenwood, 1993): 151–172.

41. *Op. cit.*: 215.

42. Herbert I. Schiller, "Public Information Goes Corporate," *Library Journal* 116 (1 Oct. 1991): 42, 45.

43. National Commission on Libraries and Information Science, "The Role of Fees in Supporting Library and Information Services in Public and Academic Libraries (April 1985)," *The Bowker Annual* 31st ed. (New York: Bowker, 1986).

44. *Ibid.*, 90–91.

45. *Ibid.*, 90.

46. *Ibid.*, 93.

47. *Ibid.*, 89.

48. John Buschman, ed., *Critical Approaches to Information Technology in Librarianship* (Westport CT: Greenwood, 1993): 134.

49. Karen Nadder Lago, "The Internet and the Public Library: Practical and Political Realities," *Computers in Libraries* 13 (Oct. 1993): 65–70.

50. John Buschman, ed., *Critical Approaches to Information Technology in Librarianship* (Westport CT: Greenwood, 1993): 135.

51. Thomas J. DeLoughry, "Unconnected," *Chronicle of Higher Education* 40 (23 Feb. 1994): A19–20.

52. Michael E. Martinez, "Access to Information Technologies Among School-Age Children: Implications for a Democratic Society," *Journal of the American Society for Information Science* 45,6 (1994): 400.

53. Scott Bennett, "The Copyright Challenge," *Library Journal* 119 (15 Nov. 1994): 34.

54. Paul Evan Peters, "Information Age Avatars," *Library Journal* 120 (15 March 1995): 33.

55. Peter R. Young, "Changing Information Economics: New Role for Libraries and Librarians," *Information Technology and Libraries* 13 (June 1994): 113–114.

56. Nancy C. Kranich, "The Selling of Cyberspace: Can Libraries Protect Public Access?" *Library Journal* 118 (15 Nov. 1993): 37.

Libraries and Poverty

BY KAREN M. VENTURELLA

My notion of democracy is that under it the weakest
should have the same opportunity as the strongest.
— Mohandas Gandhi

I once taught an adult literacy class at a Philadelphia settlement house. One of my students (an older woman) told me that she was motivated to learn to read because each year she found there to be less religious programming on television. She wanted to be able to read about her God. This book is not about literacy but it does try to speak to people's desire to change their lives and the responsibility of social institutions to provide opportunities for people to change.

Nearly 40 million U.S. citizens now live below the poverty level. Children are the fastest growing segment of the poor. Twenty-three percent of children under six years of age in this nation are living in poverty and 40 percent of the 37 million individuals living below the poverty level are under 18.[1]

What does the increasing numbers of people living in poverty mean for libraries? To borrow from Fay Blake in *Libraries, Coalition and the Public Good*, "It's the dispossessed, often lacking the means to find what they can use, whom we must help by reeducating ourselves, our communities, our friends; by developing programs for people who 'never come near the library'; and by seeking their knowledge and advice. This may open a new and exciting professional life for us."[2] In 1990, the American Library Association affirmed a "Library Service for the Poor" policy emphasizing the need for libraries to "recognize their role in enabling poor people to participate fully in a democratic society."[3]

29

Read any newspaper and you will find articles on the growth in technology and resources available electronically. But what do these changes mean for the poor? Susan Lehman Keitel, the executive director of the New York Public Library Association, warns: "What is the price of failing to act? Information injustice. The risk is information 'haves and have nots.' The information-rich, those who can pay for their information, will outpace the rest of us who may depend on the services a library can give."[4]

As a librarian, I believe that information is power and that I could use my library skills to empower others and ensure access to information for all regardless of economic level. Libraries and librarians need to look at our policies and ask ourselves how they impact all of our patrons, including the poor. For example fees for library services and overdue fines are a burden to those with low funds. "Barriers to library services may not be physical or psychological, but economic. Fines for overdue books are rarely seen as a barrier to library services, but for someone with a very low income they can be exactly that."[5] A major obstacle for homeless people is when libraries require proof of residency in order to issue a library card. San Francisco, and many other, public libraries had to struggle for the right of homeless patrons to use a shelter address as proof of residency.

I once interviewed some homeless men in Philadelphia about their experiences using the public libraries of Philadelphia. They mentioned the difficulty they used to have in obtaining library cards before the city allowed the homeless to use a shelter address for proof of residency. They also wanted to see book displays focusing on minorities — specifically, they wanted to see a display of African American reading materials. They said for the most part they had not been hassled in the library and found it to be a comfortable and safe place. I thought their requests were very simple. In my opinion, libraries have more of a responsibility to the poor than simply being "safe places."

In researching a paper titled "The Homeless and the Public Library," I came across an article by Pat Woodrum about her experiences as the director of the Tulsa (Oklahoma) Public Library. The Library had seen an increase in the number of homeless using the library as a safe haven. Pat Woodrum's response was to organize community groups to provide a more beneficial place for the homeless to go in the day. The community was able to establish the Tulsa Day Center for the homeless (funded by private sources), where homeless people can take a shower, get snacks, seek counseling and medical attention, and use the resources of a special library collection. The Tulsa Public Library was an incredible example of how libraries, in partnership with other community organizations, could serve the needs of the community. There are numerous examples of how libraries in partnership with other organizations are able to address the needs of low income groups. In a survey on homeless children in public libraries, 96 percent of librarians surveyed agreed on the importance of libraries interacting with other agencies.[6]

The Social Responsibilities Round Table (SRRT) of the ALA formed a Task Force on Hunger, Homelessness, and Poverty to foster a greater awareness of the dimensions, causes, and ways to end hunger, homelessness, and poverty, as well as a better recognition of the library/poverty nexus. SRRT's Task Force on Hunger, Homelessness, and Poverty, along with the Intellectual Freedom Round Table; and the Progressive Librarians Guild, sponsored a program titled "Poor People and Libraries: What's the Connection?" at the ALA annual conference in New York City in July 1996. The task force sponsored a program on fees as barriers to access at the 1977 ALA conference. These programs focus the profession on the need to provide access and service to all patrons.

I believe libraries have the responsibility to be responsive to the needs of the communities that they serve. The poor are constituents of that community. Nancy Harvey Davis and Pam Fitzgerald, in an article titled "Libraries and the Homeless," list many actions libraries can take to be "an aggressive part of solutions to homelessness." I would extend their suggestions to apply not only to the homeless but to all poor people.

> They (libraries) can provide vital community and social service referral information; job search and career guidance; and educational/vocational course information. They can keep on hand a variety of job applications and tax forms as well as driver's license applications; first aid, dietary, AIDS, and other healthcare information; sample check books; magazines and children's books to give away; sample ballots; and current classified and help wanted sections. Librarians can assemble collections that can be taken into the streets — and into shelters, welfare hotels, Head Start programs, and food kitchens. Libraries can band together with social services to create "crisis literacy" programs that provide strategies for managing a bureaucratic maze or instructions on filling out complicated forms."[7]

Numerous Library Programs

The programs described in this book in no way offer a complete picture of the numerous programs offered by libraries to serve the needs of the poor. Many programs focus on the needs of homeless individuals but by extension can include economically disadvantaged individuals. Some programs focus on referral, some programs bring books to shelters, some provide job assistance and referral; there are many other forms of assistance as well.

The Enoch Pratt Free Library, in cooperation with the Baltimore County Coalition for the Homeless, provides a "Street Card" listing various services available to those in need. The Memphis/Shelby County (Tennessee) Public Library operates a referral service to aid the homeless. The Detroit Public Library created a TIP ("The Information Place") Community Resource Database for use by human service professionals in referring clients to basic services; it lists agencies and over 100 specific services. This program is funded in part by a Library Services and Construction Act FY1992 Title One grant from the library of Michigan awarded to the Detroit Associated Libraries.

Multnomah (Oregon) County Public Library and Milwaukee Public Library are two systems that received special federal grants to go to shelters and other centers where the homeless sleep to provide collections of self-help material and books and magazines for their use. San Francisco Public Library provides similar services from locally-generated funds. The public library in Haverhill, Massachusetts, set up a special community room for the homeless that has books, magazines, and newspapers as well as information on community social services. The Saint Paul Public Library serves all residents living at a local shelter, using the shelter as the person's address to issue a library card. The Loaves and Fishes Center, a private, not-for-profit agency that offers free lunches and shelter, and provides showers, laundry and bathrooms in Sacramento, California, opened a library and reading room for the homeless. The library was opened because directors of the program saw a different kind of hunger on the streets that was not being met.[8]

Families waiting to apply for aid from the Hennepin County Family Assistance Division can spend their time watching videotapes that encourage reading in the home and then select a book from an on-site collection to read aloud to their children while they wait. This is a service operated by the Hennepin County Library. A Spokane Public Library Education/Job Information Center provides homeless individuals with career testing and job search information, and provides job search assistance, including résumé preparation, help with interviewing and job search strategies, and information on educational opportunities, and opportunities for career evaluation and exploration.

Other amazing discoveries I made in doing my research was a Libraries for the Future proposal for public libraries to play a supportive role in providing preventive health care information and referral services for homeless women, families, and children. Molly McQuade, a *Booklist* correspondent, reported on a homeless man named Tim Donohue, who wrote a book titled *In the Open* using his local library in Henderson, Nevada. Donohue credited the library with enabling him to complete his book: "If it hadn't been for the library, and for the word processors there — which you can use almost for free — I probably wouldn't have been able to write the book."[9]

Professional Considerations

I wish I could say that it is the noble history of libraries to be institutions designed to serve the poor. But Michael Harris and others have shown libraries through history have not always been motivated by service to society.[10] The library profession does not agree on the extent to which librarians should become involved in social issues. In the June 1994 issue of *American Libraries*, there was a debate on this issue. One side of the debate was titled "Telescopic Philanthropy: How Much Social Responsibility Is Too Much?" and the other side was titled "The Clear Imperative for Involvement: Librarians Must Address Social Issues."[11] It is my personal and professional belief that libraries and librarians, whether working in a building called a library or in the street or through a neighborhood coalition or community group, need to address the poverty that pervades society.

In the words of E.J. Josey in speaking about homeless patrons, "These people are not problem patrons, they are patrons in need of your help, because you are a civilizing agency. The library has the power to help them and as librarians you have the power to help forge coalitions that will serve not only the homeless, but also the best interest of your city and your library."[12]

It is a moral imperative that we be responsive to the needs of the community and provide opportunities for people to change their lives. I remember a great bookmark created by the American Library Association that had the motto, "Libraries Change Lives." I believe this is true. Much of what I read in compiling this book gives me hope. The public library programs designed to reach low income groups, especially children, who are the fastest growing segment of the poor, are prevalent and are having a positive effect on many people's lives.

Notes

1. Leatha Lamison-White, "Poverty in the United States: 1996," *Current Population Reports* (Washington, D.C.: U.S. Dept. of Commerce, Sept. 1997): vi.
2. E.J. Josey, ed., *Libraries, Coalition and the Public Good* (New York: Neal-Schuman, 1987): 21.

3. American Library Association, "Library Services for the Poor," in *ALA Handbook of Organization* (Chicago: ALA, 1996): 139–140.

4. Susan Lehman Keitel in *Viewpoints* (New York Public Library, May 1995): A24.

5. Joshua Cohen and Mary M. Flad. "Reinventing the Image of the Public Library," *Multicultural Review* 6, 2 (June 1997): 50.

6. Francis Smardo Dowd, "Homeless Children in Public Libraries: A National Survey of Large Systems," *Journal of Youth Services in Libraries* 9 (Winter 1996): 155–66.

7. Nancy Harvey David and Pam Fitzgerald, "Libraries and the Homeless," *Library Journal* 118 (1 March 1993): 27.

8. Kathleen Grubb, "Library for Homeless Fills a Mental Need," *San Jose Mercury News* (14 Nov. 1993): 5.

9. Molly McQuade, "Writing a Book at the Library," *Booklist* 93 (15 Oct. 1996): 383.

10. Michael Harris, "The Purpose of the American Public Library: A Revisionist Interpretation of History," *Library Journal* 98 (15 Sept. 1973): 2509–2514.

11. William Uricchio, "Telescopic Philanthropy: How Much Social Responsibility Is Too Much?" and John Buschman, Mark Rosenzweig and Elaine Harger, "Clear Imperatives for Involvement: Librarians Must Address Social Issues," *American Libraries* 25 (June 1994): 574–76.

12. E.J. Josey, "Libraries, Coalitions and the Homeless," address delivered at the 1986 Annual Conference of ALA, New York City.

POVERTY PROGRAMS FOR CHILDREN

"Reading Can Give You a Dream"

BY PAM CARLSON

In 1989, Orange County Public Library applied to the California State Library for a Library Services and Construction Act grant. The purpose: to provide library services to the residents of Orangewood Children's Home, the county's largest emergency shelter for children who have been removed from their homes as a result of abuse (physical or sexual), neglect, or abandonment. Orangewood serves almost 3,000 children each year, ranging in age from newborn to 18. Its demographics are a reflection of Orange County's population, mostly white and Hispanic, followed by Asian and African American. Currently, the daily resident average at the Home is close to 300 children.

Orangewood, created with a combination of county and private funding, is not your stereotypically drab shelter. Spanish-style cottages with tile roofs house the children, who are grouped by age and sex. There is a year-round, on-grounds school run by the Orange County Department of Education for grades K–12, a preschool program, and a variety of regular recreational activities to keep the kids occupied and happy during their stay. The cottages have large-screen TVs and videocassette players, and are stocked with donated books for children to read if they choose and are able to read. Not surprisingly, most of the children are functioning below grade level in school, but many still have a desire to learn. What better way to help fulfill this desire than to provide a structured library program?

As a library specialist, I was hired to lead "Library S*T*A*R*S (Story Times, Activities and Reading in Shelters)." The first year was funded by the grant, and a full-time library assistant worked with me. We began our project by doing research to see if there were any other library programs in children's or family shelters across the country. We found many librarians and volunteers who visited shelters to conduct storytimes, and several shelters that made donated books available to their charges. One shelter actually had a school library, but it apparently went unused during non-school hours. Nowhere were we able to find any other attempt to duplicate the services of a public library in a shelter facility.

After visiting Orangewood and talking to the staff, we decided that the children would benefit most if we offered them the same types of programs we would hold in any public library. We followed the traditional "reading calendar" by recognizing Children's Book Week and National Library Week, and by conducting a summer reading program. Our storytimes included crafts and other reading reinforcement activities aimed at our target age group of five to 12 year olds.

To complement the programs, we borrowed books from other OCPL branches, and made these available to the kids. We also organized the collections in the cottages to make them age appropriate, and purchased many new titles. Some of the grant money was used to purchase books to give away to children to "keep forever." For many, this was the first book they had ever owned. By the end of the first year, the program had expanded beyond the original target group to include preschoolers and high school students. We bought books for the latter to read during their free time, and for staff to use during group teaching times. We had accomplished our goals and then some.

The original plan for the second and subsequent years was to have OCPL branch staff continue to provide library programs at Orangewood on a rotating basis. This did in fact happen for several months, with both children's and adult library specialists (and even some branch managers) presenting a variety of programs. However, it soon became obvious that even the most well-intentioned programs could not take the place of a permanent librarian at the Home. Her presence would insure consistency for children not used to much stability, and would also guarantee the presence of someone familiar with this population's reading needs and interests who could build a collection based on those needs.

Orange County Public Library agreed to supply the staff (one library specialist), a budget for books, periodicals and supplies, and computers to access the library's catalog and circulation system. Orangewood provided a room for the library and the cost of telephone lines to connect the Home with the library's database. Shelving was donated and installed by the Burt C. Gentle Company. The Home also has two fundraising groups, which agreed to support summer reading and other library projects.

Since the Orangewood library uses the same Dynix library automation system as do the other county branches, users have complete computer access to the vast OCPL collection. Books here are arranged in the same manner as in any other public library: nonfiction by Dewey class, fiction by the author's last name. That way, students can transfer the library skills they learn at Orangewood to libraries in the community; they have confidence in their ability to use libraries after they leave the Home.

I use a variety of methods to encourage Orangewood kids to become readers. I visit the older babies in the nursery once a week with a bag of board books. Usually these are chewed upon by the members of the "Baby Literary Society," but there are also oohs and aahs from those who find the pictures inside. I also take books to the toddler cottage to read aloud. This is obviously not the usual toddler storytime, with each child sitting on a parent's lap doing finger plays and hearing stories. Instead, participants each choose a book and loudly ask me to read them all at the same time while everyone attempts to sit on my lap—a bit of a reading free-for-all. But it seems to work, and the kids look forward to these times.

Preschoolers through sixth graders visit the library weekly with their teachers for storytimes and to check out books. Each classroom and cottage has a library card that all its members use to borrow materials. A weekly bedtime storytime is held for ages 5–8 in their cottage, while boys and girls ages 9–11 visit the library every other week after school for specially planned programs. The junior high girls and boys come on alternate weeks for books and crafts. High schoolers visit when the mood strikes and staff bring them, but the teachers are planning to begin weekly class visits.

Obviously, at Orangewood there is a wide range of reading interests. Expectant teens want books on pregnancy with lots of pictures. Those who are here with their babies spend a lot of time caring for them. Some want to read to their babies, and of course they are encouraged to do so. We have purchased a Reading Is Fundamental program called "Shared Beginnings," an easy-to-use program with activities and suggestions geared to young parents. Some of the activities and suggestions have been implemented.

Poetry is popular with the teens, especially love poems which can be copied and sent to boyfriends or girlfriends. All ages ask for drawing books, books about animals, mysteries, and horror. Series books such as the Hardy Boys and Babysitters Club circulate frequently, just as they do at any other library serving children. Oversize books are also popular. I think they are regarded as status symbols; that is, the larger the book, the better the reader. So, sometimes, I'll see kids with little reading ability lugging around great big books. Fortunately, most of these books also have lots of pictures so there is something to hold the user's interest.

Many on-going and special events round out the Orangewood residents' library experience. "Superb Storytellers" was started when the preschoolers began visiting the library. This group involves two or three older children at a time, who read stories to and put on puppet shows for the preschoolers. The storytellers are not necessarily top students, but they have a desire to "work with the little kids." The unexpected often happens here: a quiet kid discovers a talent for creating lively puppet voices; an unsure reader gains confidence while reading a repetitive text; preschoolers actually sit still while their siblings and friends read to them. Preschoolers themselves will imitate the readers, holding up books, and "reading" to the others, remembering to show the pictures. Each "Superb Storyteller" is rewarded with a certificate and candy bar. For some, this is the first recognition of the fact that the ability to read is a valuable skill to have. That they have this skill is a great thing to realize for kids who may not have many other things going for them.

We receive many donated books, especially at Christmas. Many are added to the collection, but others are given away to the children to keep. I use some as prizes for game times. It's very easy to play "The Price Is Right" and have the students bid on books trying to guess the "actual retail price," the number of pages, or year the book was published. Once, several books without covers were donated by a bookstore. This gave us an opportunity to have kids to design their own covers.

Because many of the young people read below grade level, I read aloud most the books shared during storytime. Sometimes, though, I will rewrite a text into a readers' theater script to give myself a break, and the kids a chance to be dramatic. A couple of times, kids have rehearsed and performed readers' theater for all of the other children. But this is tough to plan because Orangewood kids come and go without advance notice, usually on the day of the performance. However, the children who took part were proud of their reading and loved the applause.

Entertainers and storytellers donate their time and talents occasionally, adding a little pizzazz to the regular library programs. We sometimes hold reading celebrations that involve all of the children. Because we are close to Disneyland, we invited Alice and the White Rabbit to attend an un-birthday party with games and food to kick off one summer reading program. They were kind enough to give out the awards for our bookmark design contest. Another time, we had a Garfield reading feast where the highlight was a rented lion costume (the closest we could get to Garfield). The older kids took turns wearing it to entertain the younger ones. We have also participated in the Pizza Hut Book-It program, holding monthly pizza parties for those who read the required number of books. Readers may also be rewarded with trips to a local miniature golf center or amusement park, using coupons donated by local businesses.

Flexibility and creativity are required when working in a facility like Orangewood, but you can do a lot of things that would not work in a regular library and experiment with new ideas. Storytime groups are fairly small — averaging between 12 and 30 — so that there is a lot of interaction between the kids and me. I can do things at this library which can't easily be done at others. For example, I make use of our kitchen. Everyone likes to eat, and learning to read recipes and cook is important, especially for kids who can't always depend on adults to do it for them. We have prepared both full dinners and snacks. Lately, the recreation director and I have combined forces to do multicultural cooking classes once or twice a month. There are plenty of stories centered around food, and making a snack to go with them reinforces what has been read. Obvious choices are making chocolate chip cookies for *If You Give a Mouse a Cookie*, or spaghetti for *Strega Nona*. For gross-out fun we used a donated "Doctor Dreadful" kit to make some truly disgusting looking (but good-tasting) ice cream, and put food coloring in 7-Up to complement a story called *Professor Puffendorf's Secret Potions*. In contrast to this, the junior high girls made English trifle at Thanksgiving.

We also go on field trips to other OCPL branches. These trips are combined with visits to attractions near the libraries. We have visited John Wayne Airport, with tours provided by county personnel and American Airlines, and nature centers, the Santa Ana Zoo, a working farm at a high school, a Victorian house, a children's museum, a mission, several parks, and the beach. Of course, you have to have lunch on a field trip. So we use donated fast food coupons or pack a picnic. At the airport, we ate Happy Meals in a passenger waiting area. The highlight of these field trips is the library visit, with a storytime provided by the branch children's librarian and the opportunity to check out books. We usually travel by van with Orangewood counselors as drivers, but have also gone on a few local train trips (the first time for most of the kids). These trips are both fun and educational for everyone involved, although a lot of work goes into the arrangements.

In addition to providing reading encouragement to young residents, the library also functions as a source of curriculum support for the school. Teachers may request titles for various course units. Class visits include a story and possibly a short game or film, often celebrating an author's birthday or happening as listed in *Chase's Annual Calendar of Events*. The library circulates approximately 1400 items per month, many of them checked out during school visits.

The library at Orangewood is a rare example of cooperation between county agencies. Housed at a Social Services facility, it is staffed and primarily funded by OCPL. It serves a school administered by the Orange County Department of Education, as well as classes at Juvenile Hall, which is part of the Probation Department.

Juvenile Hall is located next door to Orangewood, and after discussion with teaching staff at the Hall, it seemed natural to extend our services to include them. Twice a week, I roll a bookcart filled with paperbacks and magazines through six classes at Juvenile Hall, where the students (mostly male) are awaiting sentencing for felony accusations. Sentences for many will be served at the Hall; others will be transferred to California Youth Authority or other institutions. The average age is about 14, but it seems as if they're getting younger.

I have noticed what seems to be a reading gap among the Hall students. Many express familiarity with books intended for middle readers — Beverly Cleary and the Indian in the Cupboard series — then reading interests jump to Sidney Sheldon, Anne Rice, and other adult books. Few kids seem to have read after the fourth grade. I'm not sure what the explanation for this is; perhaps it is due to a disinterest in school, to trouble at home which takes the focus off of learning, or involvement in other activities, such as gangs. Many of the young men say that, because they are required to spend much of the day in their rooms, they have the time to really read for the first time in their lives. As they become familiar with authors and titles, they recommend and book-talk them to each other. "Hey, check out this book. This Dean Koontz (or Stephen King or Lois Duncan or Joan Nixon) is a good writer." Someone who comes in already a reader can introduce his favorites to the others, who are willing to read new (to them) titles. Several want to re-read the old books they knew from elementary school. We can satisfy most of their needs because we can request books from other libraries, as long as they are available in paperback. For security purposes, hardbound books are perceived as possible weapons. But even these may sometimes be supplied, with the permission of staff.

We have had successful programs, even at Juvenile Hall. High schoolers took part in "A Slice of Life" mystery lunch. Each boy received a "menu" listing nine book and magazine titles and authors. They numbered them in any order and were served three items at a time. Each title or author represented a different food, silverware, or condiment. For one course, a student might be served dessert, a drink, and catsup after ordering "Dean

Koontz, Mad magazine, and *Don't Look Behind You.*" The lessons learned from this exercise were that, just as you never know in advance what will happen in life, you have no clue as to what you will be served during this meal. You can get more if you ask nicely. And there are always adults who just help themselves to the food without asking.

For the past year, students at our next door Interim Care Facility have also come to the library on a weekly basis. The teens housed there are mainly Orangewood "graduates" and are familiar with the library from time spent here. The difference is that they are now older and given more choices and freedom in what they can read. The group is smaller than the average Orangewood gathering, and more individual attention can be given. They have learned how to use the computer to search for books and do their own requests.

The library program would not be successful without encouragement and support from the Orangewood staff. In the beginning, many were skeptical. "Kids here don't read, they have no interest in books," was the main comment we heard from counselors and social workers. Were they ever surprised when they saw how enthusiastically the children responded to library time! Now, staff who were closet readers encourage the kids in their reading habits by checking out their favorite stories to read aloud during quiet times. They also assist by returning books to the library when a child is released, and help with crowd control during storytimes.

The Orangewood Library is the little library that could — year after year, for eight years so far, despite such obstacles as OCPL-wide budget shortages that limited library services here to one day a week for approximately six months, while I did double duty as children's librarian both here and at another branch. Other problems? Sure, we've got a few. Books and magazines that are taken by children when they leave Orangewood add up to about thirty missing items each month. Some materials are torn up by frustrated children during angry moments. And because the library doubles as a crafts room, some volunteer leaders assume that I am in charge of providing materials and will clean up after the event (but we're working on this one). The population of Orangewood is intended to be transient, so projects and programs can't last long or most kids won't be around to complete them. On the other hand, programs which went over well the first time can be recycled without complaint.

The library is also a source of consistency and continuity as kids come, go, and return when a placement doesn't work out. Older ones who used the library when they were younger can find the books they read then, and either re-read them as familiar friends, or explore new titles. One teen girl told me she regarded the library as a haven from chaos, and would come here just to hang out when things got rough. Remember, these kids are together 24 hours a day with others they probably would not have chosen as friends on the outside — when trouble erupts, there aren't many places to escape from it.

Reading offers choices. The necessary shelter structure of working with children as groups can be hard on individual desires. But one can choose what one wants to read. After consultation with the staff, we have restricted young adult and adult materials to the older teens. Everyone, though, is exhorted to read what they have the ability to understand and enjoy, for the pure joy of reading without any pressure to seek information, or for any other goal imposed by another. We want to get across the idea that reading is a valuable skill in life, but it's also fun; an opportunity to escape from life's problems for a little while.

I try to stress the role of libraries as important resources so that visiting them will become a habit. Through a library's books and other materials, children can discover much about themselves, and the rest of the world. The title for this article was taken from a statement made by one of the students at Juvenile Hall and remains true today: "Reading can give you a dream" wherever you are.

At Work in
the Children's Room

BY KHAFRE K. ABIF, OMO OBATALA

Beginning with some background on the current social situation in the United States, this chapter describes library programs, both at Montclair Public Library and the District of Columbia Public Library, that focus on low-income populations. It is important that the reader have some sense of my professional approach. The following (from an essay published in 1996) expresses the philosophy I bring to my work as a youth services librarian and program coordinator:

> Our results will breathe life into the eyes of our children and prepare them for a meaningful life that shines brightly with a promising future of hope. No longer will we have to ask ourselves: Why are our children not educated? Why are our children dying at such an unbelievable rate? Whose knowledge is most valuable for the development of Afrikan* children and youth? Why do I kill myself and others who look like me? Do I love myself and those who look like me? Are Afrikan ideas crucial to our discourse and development? Can an Afrikan really be multicultural if he/she does not first have his/her culture? At what age do children cease to smile naturally, smile full teeth, uninhibited smiles? Where does childhood stop in many of our communities? How many killings, rapes, beatings, verbal and mental abuse, hustles, get-over programs, drug-infested homes, parents and communities, drive-by shootings/drive-by leaders must they witness before their eyes dry up for good and their only

*I spell the word "Afrika" because for many activists the "k" represents an acknowledgment that "Africa" is not the true name of that vast continent. When I speak of Afrika, it is from an Afrikan-centered viewpoint. Therefore, Afrika with a "k" represents a redefined and potentially different Afrika, and also it symbolizes for me a coming back together of Afrikan people worldwide. Let it be understood that when I speak of Afrika and when most whites think of "Africa," we are coming from two different worldviews.[1]

thought is: "Will I make it to the age of twenty-five?" A Marvin Gaye song from years past echoes my commitment. Let's save the children ... all of the children ... live life for the children ... save the babies.[2]

The most telling indictment of recent American social policy is that it has left children poorer. In 1969 the U.S. Census Bureau estimated that 14 percent of America's children were poor; this compares with 20.8 percent in 1995. Despite the healthy economy, America's youth remain the poorest among us and their numbers are soaring. Some 6.1 million children under age six, nearly the population of Chicago and Los Angeles combined, lived in poverty in 1994. That is one in four kids, a proportion unmatched among the world's industrialized nations. This nation's Afrikan American children are hit the hardest when it comes to poverty, with a larger percentage of Afrikan American children living in extreme poverty than the percentage of European American children.[3]

The condition of the inner-city Afrikan American poor is a painful domestic problem. How such misery can exist in one of the richest countries in the world is a question foreigners have long asked embarrassed Americans. No other major industrial nation has allowed its cities to face the types of fiscal and social troubles, particularly the deep concentration of poverty, that confront America's cities. America's cities are in decay and we can see the consequences of inattention every day. The symptoms of poverty serve as the landscaping of the inner-city: declining living standards, homelessness, infant mortality, violent crime, segregation, crumbling infrastructure, fiscal trauma, corporate flight and economic restructuring, suburban exodus, redlining, and federal cutbacks. Each symptom contributes to the growing American underclass.

Can this condition be explained by the inherent racism of European Americans? Or perhaps by the fact that the manufacturing jobs that once sustained poorly educated Afrikan American Southern migrants have been moved out of urban centers? And thus, there follow all the associated ills of the Afrikan American inner city. There may be a connection between what people expect or hope to earn in jobs and the jobs available. Economists call it the "reserve wage." What Afrikan Americans are willing to work for is higher than the reserve wage of less educated immigrants. "The immigrants' social origins predisposed them to embrace jobs that native New Yorkers would no longer accept; meager as they appeared to New Yorkers, the paychecks in the city's garment, restaurant, or retail sectors looked good in comparison to the going rate in Santo Domingo, Hong Kong, or Kingston."[4]

Afrikan Americans who have gained advanced education or skills have moved out of the ghetto in large numbers. But many have been left behind at a time when relatively low-skilled and poorly educated immigrants have been pouring into the old immigrant cities, in part because of the passage of the 1965 Immigration Reform Act. Nathan Glazer suggests that this contrast between the Afrikan American poor and the new low-skilled immigrants undermines the "mismatch" theory of the condition of inner-city Afrikan Americans who may believe that the jobs they can fill have left the city and that they are unequipped for the jobs that remain. He believes there is a different mismatch that provides a better explanation.

> This mismatch, which emerged in the late 1960s, before the new immigrant wave grew to its present proportions, was between black expectations regarding what constituted suitable work and suitable wages and what was available. These expectations may well have been fully understandable in the wake of three centuries of slavery and Jim Crow, and at a time when powerful civil rights laws were passed and agencies to enforce them were created. But this past did not change the calculations of employers as they came across applicants who expected more than they could offer and were resentful at what was provided.[5]

Glazer suggests that the applicants' parents, the migrants from the South, had been prepared to take the poor jobs, and that in this respect, they were like the earlier uneducated European immigrants, or the lower skilled immigrants from Asia and Latin America who began arriving after the 1965 reforms. However the children of Southern migrants expected better. Better was not available because of the insufficiencies of their education. Their disappointment and outrage made them poor prospects for the available low level jobs. Subsequently, new immigrants received the low level jobs. Around the same time, 1964 and 1965, both the civil rights laws and the new immigration law that abolished quotas and racial preference were fulfilling a great American promise. Laws passed with the intention of opening opportunity to all without consideration of race or ethnicity, ironically, widened the gates to immigration, which helped in turn to undermine the promise of the civil rights law. A case could be made that in the absence of new immigrants, employers might have raised the wages of the jobs they had, and the real wages might then have come closer to matching the "reserve wage" of the children of the Afrikan American Southern migrants.

This is the second time this scenario has played out. Afrikan Americans were already on the bottom rungs of economic advancement when W.E.B. Du Bois studied the Philadelphia Negro in the 1890s.[6] These Afrikan Americans saw themselves being pushed off those rungs by European immigrants, whom European Americans preferred as employees or providers of services. The same story holds true in New York, as Herman D. Bloch showed in his study of Afrikan Americans in New York.[7] These may be factors as to why Afrikan American male unemployment rates have remained more than twice as high as European American rates throughout the past three decades. Simple prejudice led employers to prefer European immigrants to Afrikan Americans. Better educated Afrikan Americans have been much more successful at obtaining jobs, often in the public sector, but the lesser educated are left out in the cold.

Not all learning takes place in the classroom. Learning must begin well before a child reaches school. Researchers have shown that 50 percent of a child's intellectual development takes place before age four. That is where our nation's public libraries have a major role. Libraries provide a wealth of books and other resources that can give every child a head start on life and learning. While reading is still the most basic survival skill in an information society, being able to read is not enough. Children must learn how to navigate the information superhighway. The most well-equipped public libraries provide books, computers and a wide range of programs to prepare young children to live and work in the coming century.

> We have long-term strategic plans for our national defense, our economy, our nation's highways and bridges. But America's kid's, our nation's most valuable resource, often get left out in the cold. To correct that problem, we must ensure that our children develop the necessary skills to formulate and pursue worthwhile goals.
>
> Public libraries play a vital role in this effort. They provide our children with confidence, stability, perspective, inspiration, and access to knowledge. They give preschoolers mental stimulation and they educate young parents, grandparents and other primary caregivers in child development. And they provide young adolescents with safe havens, role models, caring adult listeners and tutoring. In short, libraries fill in the gaps that exist in many kids' lives. Providing comprehensive support for libraries is critical to preparing America's children to work, parent and govern in the 21st century.[8]

The public library customer base begins with children. If we, in the children's room, plant the right seed today we will grow lifelong learners. Preparing our children to become adults in the 21st century, the age of information, will determine the success of American society in the coming generations. A paper prepared by the Association of College and Research Libraries, the Association for Library Services to Children, and other divisions of the American Library Association provides goals and examples for achieving school readiness in America's children. *Implementing the National Goals for Education Through Library Services* states that libraries have a significant impact on a person's life and learning. Programs and services are already in place at home, at school, and in the workplace, helping people to maximize their potential for learning and self-realization. The paper states as its major goal that by the year 2000 all children in America will start school ready to learn.[9] Librarians and library programs work with children, parents and other adults to provide materials and pre-reading experiences that prepare children to enter and remain in school. Examples of effective library programs can be found throughout the country. The paper details several: public libraries offer programs to introduce toddlers and preschoolers to books, to the library and to multimedia resources in the library; library programs for the very young provide a positive environment for developing social skills needed in formal education; libraries work with parents and caregivers to provide multimedia materials and experiences and an enticing atmosphere to develop reading interest. Children, parents and staff of child care centers, Head Start and other prekindergarten programs use materials, deposit collections and programming provided by public libraries; literacy programs in public libraries provide basic skills training for parents and other caregivers; public librarians offer training and guidance to parents and caregivers on preparing their children for reading.

In my experience as youth services librarian in the children's room I have witnessed the success of library programming that reaches children and families where they are. I would always encourage the public library community to find ways to expand its service, even in the face of budget restraints, to reach underserved populations. Many immigrant youth have learned to read in America's public libraries, thus paving the way for the future success of their family. Literacy has become increasingly more important in this information society. Communication, literacy and technical skills are essential for fruitful life pursuits. The literate have control over their own destiny: "Information is power."

The mission of the Montclair Public Library is to act as a focal institution and system for publicly supported access by individuals to information, knowledge and reading in Montclair. The trustees believe that citizens deserve quality services and access to information-based technology. In a multicultural environment, the library strives to act as a center for life-long learning for all citizens, and particularly for its young people; and as a facilitator, organizer and provider of information about the community and local government.

In keeping with these goals, the Montclair Public Library has offered a literacy program for adults since 1987. The Family Learning program is a key component of the literacy program. Historically, the library has long had a collaborative arrangement with the Montclair Child Development Center (Head Start), which serves the communities of Montclair and Orange, New Jersey.

Head Start was launched by the federal government in 1965 to help young children from low-income families get a better start in life. Aimed primarily at three to five year olds, it is a comprehensive child development program that fosters learning, better health, active parental involvement and family self-sufficiency. Today over 721,000 children and families are served by Head Start programs each year. There are 322 Head Start families of which 79 are single, female head of household, and 70 percent are AFDC recipients aged 19 to 30. A small number of families are headed by grandparents who have assumed child rearing responsibilities for grandchildren.

The Library–Head Start Partnership Project continues a cooperative effort that began in 1989 with a symposium on "Learning Opportunities for Children: Libraries and Their Partners," which was cosponsored with the Association for Library Services to Children (ALSC). The project is administered through a joint agreement between the Center for the Book in the Library of Congress and the Head Start Bureau of the U.S. Department of Health and Human Services. The project is being carried out with the collaboration of ALSC, a division of the 55,000 member American Library Association. The project is designed to demonstrate in communities nationwide how libraries that serve young children can plan and work with Head Start grantees/classrooms to enhance learning and parent involvement in children's literacy and language development.

Beginning in 1993, the Montclair Public Library experimented successfully with bringing family-oriented evening programs to the Head Start facility as a part of our Summer Reading Club. Out of that venture came joint sponsorship of a literacy program offering adult basic education and GED tutoring as well as programming directed to families. More recently we have sought to expand our Family Learning program to operate throughout the year in conjunction with our Adult Literacy tutoring. The Montclair Public Library strives to meet the literacy and human development needs of low-literate adults and their families, especially in the educationally under-served community. In February 1994 the Montclair Public Library targeted youth services and technology-based services as focal points of the Library's overall service plan. A key component of the youth services long range plan is to provide support to parents and caregivers in their role as the child's first teacher. A successful Family Learning program is essential to bringing library services to a chronically under-served population. This program will permit the library to increase and expand its offerings in the areas of literacy training or tutoring of adults, together with literacy-related activities for children.

To share a story using children's literature as the foundation for Family

Learning is the approach I have used to build the literacy of children and their families. The goals and objectives for the Family Learning program are:

- To connect parents with their families through literacy-building activities and parenting skill development.
- To provide potential adult literacy students a program in their own neighborhood. Traveling to other communities to meet educational needs is difficult or impossible for people on fixed incomes, or parents with child care concerns, or people afraid to travel after dark.
- To increase the literacy skills of adult learners by at least one grade level per year.
- To ensure that the adult learners and their children have valid library cards.
- To orient and familiarize adult learners and their children to the variety of resources, materials and services available at the Montclair Public Library, including instruction in how to use the library (e.g., bibliographic instruction, reference materials, information technology).
- To provide literacy-related projects and activities for children whose parents or guardians are participating in adult literacy instruction.
- To increase participants' use of the Montclair Public Library.
- To encourage adult learners and their children to participate in at least three "Take a Book" programs.

Methods for Achieving Goals of the Project

The Family Learning program offers "Share a Story" seminars for adults and "Take a Book" seminars for both caregivers and children. The adult seminars focus on discussions of literacy-building techniques, child development and developmentally appropriate parenting practices. For the interactive family seminars, caregivers and children participate in activities such as individual and group reading or dramatizations. Children's literature is the basis of the project curriculum, integrating the parenting, child development and literacy-building components of the program. Children's books are used to raise parenting issues during instructional seminars. The instructor facilitates discussion of these issues and provides child development information as appropriate. The participants also consider how they might read this story with their children, what literacy-building activities might accompany the reading, and what questions they might ask during the reading.

By using children's literature as the basis of adult instruction, the project encourages parents to pass on this experience to their children. An information exchange at home at an early age is an important building block for learning to read.

"Take a Book" sessions feature storytelling, bringing stories to life and dramatizations. They are intended to reinforce and to extend what adults have learned in hands-on sessions with children. They are also intended to put books into the hands and homes of children to keep. Owning books and having them easily available in the home plays an important part both in learning to read and in valuing reading. Unfortunately, many children in our target population do not have books of their own, simply because their parents cannot afford to buy them. The "Take a Book" programs work to change this situation so that children have books to keep, learn from and enjoy again and again. Each take-home package includes two books, a candy cane or chocolate, a small age appropriate toy (cars, stuffed animals, coloring book and crayons, dinosaurs, etc.), and a flyer for parents about adult learning classes.

This approach is successful for several reasons. Adults are provided with a neutral forum for their discussions about parenting and problems may be addressed without personal disclosure. Children's literature also deals with complex and important childhood and family issues with an economy of language that is less intimidating for adults with a low literacy level. Therefore, adult learners of varying abilities are able to practice reading, questioning, and discussion skills during the seminars. Adult learning is centered around the same medium they will use to foster the child's learning and parents are introduced to the child's perspective, a point of view that enhances communication across the generations. For some parents sharing children's books is an experience they may have missed in their own childhood. Finally, the program is offered in a setting participants are already familiar with and where they feel respected and comfortable, which is important in enhancing their trust in the goals of the program and their willingness to participate.

Male Involvement Component (MIC) is an extension of the Montclair Child Development Center Head Start, which currently serves 322 families and children in the Township of Montclair and the City of Orange. The purpose of the group is two fold: to provide a way in which fathers and significant other men may play an active role in supporting the center's activities, and to organize fundraising events to help defer the costs of taking the children to organized sporting and entertainment events.

The group, organized by Umar Knox and Celester Barnes, is a way that the men would be able to take an even more active role in the mental and educational development of the children who attend the center. The Male Involvement Component has raised money to take students of the center to local sporting and educational events, and assisted and purchased turkeys during Thanksgiving. MIC puts positive role models into action, assisting not just an individual child but many children at the Head Start program.

The argument for Prison-Based Family Literacy project stems from the fact that a high percentage of residents of correctional facilities have not completed high school and many have scored below ninth grade level on achievement tests. Many of these adults and their non-incarcerated partners are not aware of or do not engage in the developmentally appropriate practices which promote children's literacy; studies show that children who spend little time with their parents in literacy-related activities have low literacy achievement, a factor which is aggravated by the incarceration of one or both parents. The structure of family visitation in correctional systems, it should be noted, does little to support literacy and parent-child bonding.

The Bureau of Justice Statistics and the Sentencing Project reported that the number of inmates in state and federal prisons increased more than fivefold from fewer than 200,000 in 1970 to more than 1,000,000 by 1994. And that was four years ago. An additional 490,000 were then being held in local jails. The number of persons on probation and parole has been growing dramatically along with institutional populations. There are now more than five million Americans incarcerated or on probation, or parole, an increase of 179 percent since 1980. Almost one in three (32 percent) young Afrikan American males aged 20 to 29 is under some type of correctional control (incarceration, probation, or parole), as is one in 15 young European American males, and one in 8 young Hispanic males. The Sentencing Project report on prisons and prisoners also says that in fiscal 1995, state and federal governments planned $5.1 billion in new prison construction, at an average cost of $58,000 for a medium security cell.[10]

The United States is first in the world in its rate of incarceration. Who is in our prisons and jails? Ninety-four percent of prison inmates are male, 6 percent female. Fifty percent of state and federal prisoners in 1993 were Afrikan American and 14 percent were Hispanic. Sixty-five percent of state prison inmates in 1991 had not completed high school; 33 percent of jail inmates in 1991 were unemployed prior to entering jail; 32 percent of jail inmates in 1991 who had been free for at least one year prior to their arrest had annual incomes of under $5,000. Sixty-eight percent of those sentenced to state prisons in 1990 were convicted of non-violent crimes, including 32 percent for drug offenses, and 31 percent for property offenses; 57 percent of jail inmates in 1989 reported they were under the influence of alcohol or drugs at the time they committed their offense. One in four jail inmates in 1989 was in jail for a drug offense, compared to one in ten in 1983; drug offenders constituted 21 percent of 1991 state prison inmates and 61 percent of 1993 federal prison inmates. Afrikan American males have an 18 percent chance of serving time in juvenile or adult prison at some point in their lives; European American males have a 3 percent chance.[11]

> Each day as I go to Court, I pass the inner-city public library branch that is no longer open to serve some of our children and youth who need it most. They need the order and the structure they could find there, the trust and concern of good librarians, the perspective on a larger world than the misery-ridden one in which they may live; the sequence, the reality of cause and effect, the confidence and sense of self-worth, the mental and emotional development which literacy could give them — none of which they have. Many would never appear before me in the Family and Juvenile Court if libraries could be there for them, to present lifestyle alternatives and better choices. Libraries must be supported at a level that would enable them to pursue this essential work.[12]

During my time with the District of Columbia Public Library, I worked with a literacy project that reaches a population which can find itself trapped in a cycle of poverty. The D.C. Family Literacy Project is a partnership of the D.C. Street Law Project of Georgetown University Law Center, the D.C. Department of Corrections, the D.C. Public Library, Push Literacy Action Now (PLAN), and First Book.[13] The projects mission is to connect incarcerated parents with their families through literacy-building activities and parenting skill development. Children's literature and book related activities are used to introduce child development issues, model developmentally appropriate activities that build literacy for children and parents, and provide affirming experiences between the incarcerated parents and their children.

The project takes a student-centered approach to teaching, a child-centered approach to parenting, and a literature-based approach to family literacy. Operating under the auspices of Georgetown University Law Center, the project's instructional component is supported by staff from the Children's Services Division of the D.C. Public Library and the expertise of other partners in the field of correctional education, parenting, adult education, and child development. With the assistance of a highly motivated core of volunteers the staff had been able to maximize their resources.

The partner institutions must have a commitment to seeking the funding necessary to support a successful project, as most of the funding has been provided through donations and grants.

The curriculum for the project contains two basic components, the literacy-building workshops for parents and the family workshops. Each component is based on appropriate works of children's literature. Discussions of the stories are used to provide a neutral forum for the analysis of what are often very sensitive and personal issues. By using children's literature to examine the problems of others, parents can identify behaviors and outcomes in an objective manner. This provides the opportunity to critique the actions and responses of fictional characters in a nonthreatening activity. Parents are allowed to explore and solve problems without having to disclose themselves or their own real or perceived shortcomings as parents. Putting children's literature at the center of both the parent workshops and interactive family workshops allows adults to experience the same type of shared reading activity which they will recreate with their own children.

The discussion of many important and powerful works of fiction can serve the purpose of providing a neutral forum, and a shared reading experience. However, the D.C. Family Literacy Project has chosen to make use specifically of children's literature for several important reasons:

1. *Quality.* Children's books have evolved into a high quality form of literature. With an economy of words, interesting and often complex stories are told. The fluidity of language coupled with excellent illustrations in many works complete the experience.
2. *Content.* The children's stories often deal with family issues, or provide the opportunity to view the world through the eyes of a child. These stories can open up a world of fantasy and imagination often forgotten by adults.
3. *Reading levels.* Attention to reading levels in children's literature helps to offer greater opportunities for low-level readers to experience success when reading, and a greater likelihood of practice with their families. Because these stories are relevant and easy to understand, they provide low literate adults with low literacy levels a chance to explore ideas in a context.
4. *Practicality.* Using children's stories as the basis for all components of our program allows us to model techniques with the same stories that parents might read with their own children. This makes the modeling more concrete and directly applicable. This is especially important for parents who have very low levels of confidence in reading, and for those who have had limited contact with children's literature.
5. *Exposure.* The wealth of truly impressive Afrikan American and multicultural children's literature which has appeared on the market in

recent years allows our participants to find characters and situations with which they can readily identify in a variety of settings. Many of our parents have commented that they never had stories like these growing up. Experience with these books exposes them to a sense of the universality of the human condition and allows them to retroactively enjoy what many of them missed growing up.

Participants in the project have embraced the experience of reading children's books as a way to relate to their own children and as a tool for improving communications within their families. Many of them are experiencing success with reading for the first time in their lives. The level of discussion among these adults about the children's stories is very sophisticated and insightful. For many of the parents, children's literature offers a chance to look back at their own experiences and to look to alternatives they can provide for their children.

Part of our success with the use of children's stories has come from the fact that the project staff accepts these works as valuable literature, and shows an enthusiasm toward the books. Participants' thoughts and comments are treated seriously, and their enjoyment of the books is encouraged enthusiastically. Neither staff nor participants believe that children's literature is being used as a primary resource because our parents aren't capable of thinking as adults. The experience of reading a children's story as an adult can be very different from that of a child reading it, but the enjoyment and emotional impact of well written children's literature has a universal appeal.

Certainly, children's literature cannot form the basis of an entire adult education program. However, the focus of this project is using literacy as a means of bonding within families, and the extensive use of children's literature as the main resource is consistent with this goal. The project does use parenting materials and child development information as a supplement to its curriculum, when appropriate. It should be noted that many of our participants are enrolled in adult learning programs at the facilities where they are housed, and that many of them become more interested in their own educational abilities as a result of participating in this program.

The program runs on a trimester system, with each trimester referred to as a cycle. Each cycle is directed by a unifying theme which provides the framework for book selections and curricular planning. The cycles form complete units, so that participants can join the project in any given trimester. The use of three guiding themes allows the project curriculum to address issues in a number of contexts, and to reintroduce ideas from different perspectives each trimester. Project curriculum also attempts to integrate major holidays and cultural events (e.g., Kwanzaa, Martin Luther

King, Jr., Birthday, Black History Month, Juneteenth) into the cyclical themes as appropriate. The three cyclic themes, the Family (Spring), the Community (Summer) and the World (Fall), are described below.

Cycle 1. The Family

Who are the members of my family?
How well do I know my family?
How much do I know about the history and make-up of my family?
How can I improve the relationships within my family?

The focus is on families' getting to know themselves and beginning to see themselves as functional units. Book choices center around families, traditional and nontraditional, the differing viewpoints of family members, and family history. They encourage family pride and unity. Activities are developed to help strengthen family bonds, and to provide families with an opportunity to take pride in themselves. A special emphasis on improving communication within families, developing family stories and rituals, recording special events in the family, and building cooperation among family members should guide the curriculum for this trimester.

Cycle 2. The Community

What does it mean to be a part of a community?
How can we create a supportive and caring community within this program?
How can I help my child succeed in the community, especially the school community?
Why is membership in a community so important to us?

This cycle is based on the Afrikan proverb, "It takes a whole village to raise a child." Greater attempts are made to build the participants into their own supportive community of families. Project curriculum is designed to help parents understand the important role they play in helping their children succeed within the community, beyond the home, and especially in school. Books, materials, and project choices are devoted to concepts of communication, responsibility, problem solving, teamwork, and school readiness.

Cycle 3. The World

What do I know about my culture and other cultures?
How can I help my children learn about diversity?

What can I learn from the stories of other cultures as well as stories from my own?

How can I expand my own and my child's point of reference?

This cycle introduces participants to a wide variety of multicultural literature and activities. Participants learn to integrate information about other cultures into their own interactions with their children. Efforts to promote empathy for the human condition in a variety of cultural contexts is the key to the success of this unit, and the use of multicultural literature allows participants to recognize themselves in stories of other people. Diversity, caring, cooperation, imagination and explorations are emphasized as positive aspects of the human community. *Washington Post* columnist Courtland Milloy writes:

Inside the Lorton Correctional Complex not long ago, some inmates were learning to read. One of their textbooks was *Wheels on the Bus*, a popular children's book. But when the men were asked to sing from the book, as children do, they balked.

"This is juvenile," one inmate protested. But they learned the song anyway, and when their children came to visit at the end of the lessons, the men performed for them.

"*The wheels on the bus go round and round, round and round...,*" they sang somewhat tentatively.

As smiles spread across the children's faces, however, the men began to sing a little louder. And as the children's eyes widened and their mouths opened in delight, the inmates became a full-throated chorus. Suddenly, the children joined in, marking the first time that many of the fathers had done anything together with their children.

By the time the song had ended, several inmates were in tears. "This is the greatest thing that has ever happened to me," one of them said.

The inmates were participating in a reading program called the D.C. Family Literacy Project, which helps incarcerated parents support literacy development in their children. It uses rhythm, music, movement and the cultural experiences of the inmates as teaching tools.

The literacy project, which is sponsored in part by the Law Center and the D.C. Public Library, utilizes developmentally appropriate learning practices, patience and respect. The goal is to get at least some African Americans off of that bottom layer.

As inmates realize that they can learn, their attitude toward life changes. They spend more time talking with each other about education. They begin to communicate more respectfully with their children and other family members. And they begin to expect that they will succeed in crime-free lives upon their release.[14]

Librarians serving children and youth have always been some of the most visionary leaders of the profession. These librarians have invented outreach, deposit collections of books and bookmobile routes in rural areas, primarily for children and their families. In the children's room is where I have chosen to empower families. Rescuing lives through literacy building. Nurturing children and imparting to them a sense of hope and belief in themselves and their future will lead to raised self-esteem, self-worth, and a measure of protection against the self-destructive behaviors and at-risk lifestyles that attracts young minds that do not have a strong sense of themselves or what their future may hold. I recognize my role in the children's room, not as a literature specialist, but rather a powerful force with the ability to direct or redirect the lives of children with encouragement, creativity, knowledge, understanding, attentiveness, hope and commitment.

Yes, I know libraries cannot solve all the problems of children and youth, but libraries can continue to be the "people's university." Libraries can build collaborative projects and programs with other child and family serving agencies which deal with nutrition, health, education and technology, and which include the use of books and other library materials. Libraries can organize workshops on parenting for particular groups such as teen mothers and fathers, grandparents, and foster parents. Libraries can connect children, youth, and families to a world beyond their community through programming. And it is my honest belief that libraries can provide family literacy sessions in which low level literate adults can practice with picture books and then read aloud to children.

Think back to pleasurable moments spent on an adult's lap listening to a story, or of bedtime, under the blanket tucked tightly in bed falling asleep to the sound of a story. These are the types of experience that we want to facilitate in the children's room. Providing parents, children and the community with positive interactions that build literacy while building the family. The two programs described above have a clear goal in mind. The goals are to break the cycle of low literacy and incarceration; to promote conscious, positive role modeling; to educate parents to become their child's first teachers; to empower children with literacy skills and with self-esteem to negotiate on their own behalf; and to instruct parents to use children's literature to teach their children and make personal connections with their children.

Public libraries will be challenged as they determine the scope and range of services they can provide. The populations served by these literacy projects have immense needs, and literacy is only one of them. We know that these adults may have low reading levels, a sense of insecurity associated with reading and academic ability, and a wealth of personal, social, economic and even chemical dependency problems which outweigh concerns about their own literacy or their children's literacy level. Just as public libraries have assisted immigrant youth with learning to read, and thus prepared the way for the future success of their family, public libraries can build literacy and build families by providing programming to make literacy-related interaction (sharing stories) between parents and children the core of children's services.

Appendix

PUBLIC LIBRARIES
EZAR JACK KEATS MINI-GRANTS
450 14th Street, Brooklyn, NY 11215

Application for $500 Mini-Grant

(1) Briefly describe the location of your library and the number, type and age of the population you serve.

The Family Learning program is a key component of the Literacy Program of the Montclair Public Library. Historically, the Library has long had a collaborative arrangement with the Montclair Child Development Center (Head Start), which serves the community of Montclair, New Jersey. Project Head Start is a demonstration program which provides comprehensive developmental services for low-income preschool children. There are 322 Head Start families. Seventy-nine percent are single, female head of household, and seventy percent are AFDC recipients, with the average age ranging between 19 to 30. (A small number of families are grandparents who have assumed child rearing responsibilities for grandchildren.) The ethnic breakdown is as follows: 75% African American, 20% Haitian, 4% Hispanic, and 1% White or other. Head Start children range in age from 2.9 years to 5 years.

(2) Describe the program for which you seek funding.

Too few at-risk children in the Montclair Public Library and Head Start collaborative have literacy support from their parents or books of their own to develop a passion for reading and learning. Without basic literacy skills and books in the home, it is more likely that children will not develop a desire to learn to read, nor have the opportunity to practice the habits and skills that make good readers. When the parents themselves have low-literacy skills, the likelihood is even greater that these children will not become skilled readers.

An Ezra Jack Keats Mini-Grant will support a special project within our Family Learning Program to teach reading and writing, and to provide children with a sense of adventure and exploration. Placing books into the homes of children will encourage more frequent library use; and lay the foundations for more parental involvement with the positive development of their children's reading habits. Our goals are to meet the literacy needs of children and their parents; help these families develop an interest in, a love for, and a habit of reading; increase the number of reading materials in the homes of low-income families; and provide additional opportunities for learning.

To accomplish these goals we will conduct story time programs in each classroom as a part of an outreach effort of the Library. The classroom visits will feature a reading of the book *Goggles*. Next we will conduct a series of writing workshops that will involve the children, parents and Head Start instructors. Each child will write and illustrate their own book. The final event will be an open house for children, parents, teachers, and residents of Montclair to witness the collaboration between the Montclair Public Library and Head Start. All who attend will have the opportunity to view the completed books and learn about the writing program and Mini-Grant project.

(3) If your program includes workshops, seminars, festivals, meetings, etc., please answer:
No. of sessions: _____   Length of session: _____   Frequency: _____
   all the same day _____   weekly _____   biweekly _____
   monthly _____   other:

(4) How many people do you expect to serve with this program? _____
Children _____   Parents _____   Others (Specify):

(5) Include a budget breakdown for the project, including a total figure, specifying how these monies will be used. IMPORTANT : FUNDS ARE NOT TO BE USED PRIMARILY FOR THE PURCHASE OF BOOKS AND TAPES, FOR GENERAL OPERATIONS, ADMINISTRATIVE COSTS, TRANSPORTATION OF THE AUDIENCE, FEES, AND THE LIKE. Failure to adhere to these restrictions is grounds for immediate rejection.

Project Budget

Books (pre-constructed for writing workshops) 50 × $2.95	$147.50
Goggles (50 × $4.95)	$247.50
Refreshments (for Open House)	$ 40.00
Decorations (for Open House)	$ 20.00
Film (5 rolls × $4 ea.)	$ 20.00
Paper Products (plates, napkins, cups)	$ 20.00
TOTAL	$495.00

Notes

1. Haki R. Madhubuti. *Black Men: Obsolete, Single, Dangerous? Afrikan American Families in Transition: Essays in Discovery, Solution and Hope* (Chicago: Third World Press, 1990): 1.
2. Khafre K. Abif, "Afrikan Centered Scholar: At Work in the Children's Room," in *In Our OWN Voices: The Changing Face of Librarianship* (Lanham, MD: Scarecrow Press, 1996): 259.
3. "About ⅓ of Black Children Live in Poverty: Study," *Jet* 91, 7 (30 Dec. 1996–1 Jan. 1997): 32.
4. Nathan Glazer. "The Hard Questions: Help Wanted," *The New Republic* 215, 4274 (16 Dec. 1996): 29
5. *Ibid.*
6. William E. B. DeBois. *The Philadelphia Negro* (Philadelphia: Pub. for the University, 1899).

7. David Bloch Herman. *The Circle of Discrimination: An Economic and Social Study of the Black Man in New York* (New York. New York University Press, 1969).

8. Virginia H. Mathews. "Kids Can't Wait...Library Advocacy Now! A President's Paper for Mary R. Somerville, President 1996-97, American Library Association" (Chicago: American Library Association, 1996): 2.

9. "Implementing the National Goals for Education Through Library Services." An unpublished report in response to the National Education Goals from the Governor's Conference. The report was developed by an American Library Association interdivisional task force chaired by Marion Rutsch. The divisions are ACRL, ALSC, ASCLA, PLA, RASD, and YASD. Pages 1–2.

10. Marc Mauer. "Young Black Americans and the Criminal Justice System: Five Years Later" (Washington, D.C.: The Sentencing Project, 1995): 1–2.

11. *Op. cit.*: 3–6.

12. Mathews, "Kids Can't Wait...A President's Paper" (1996): 2.

13. Richard L. Roe. "Voices Focus: The D.C. Family Literacy Project," *Georgetown Journal on Fighting Poverty* 2, 2 (Spring 1995): 285–300.

14. Courtland Milloy. "Literacy's Pass Key to Freedom: Reading Their Way Out of Cages," *Washington Post*, March 19, 1993, B1 & b4, col. 1.

Denver Public Library Reads Aloud to Young Children

BY SHARON MORRIS

Library outreach programs are especially important for children who might not otherwise have access to any literacy experiences at all, such as homeless children or those living in public care facilities. In addition to being at an education disadvantage, these children have a great need for some of the emotional benefits that early literacy activities can provide, such as the development of self-esteem and a sense of belonging and social acceptance.[1]

The other day, a six-year-old Hispanic girl was roaming the Denver Public Library with a smile on her face and her library card in hand. She explained that she had gotten the card the year before when she was at Head Start. When her father and young brother were ready to leave, she held up the library card and said, "Come on, Dad. I'll pay for the books."

This girl is one of thousands of children who have been introduced to the library through the Denver Public Library Read-Aloud Program. The outreach reading program extends into low-income neighborhoods where children may not have as many opportunities to visit the library. The Read-Aloud Program relies on volunteers who visit homeless and abuse shelters, low-income daycare centers such as Head Starts, and the Children's Hospital oncology floor. Each volunteer reader "adopts" a classroom for ten weeks. They visit the classroom to read stories to the children, give them their first library card, and offer meaningful experiences with books. Shelters are served throughout the year, while Head Starts and other nonprofit daycare centers participate for one of the quarterly sessions. Over 1,200 preschool children participate each week with nearly 5,000 served throughout the year. Through this outreach program, DPL brings the library to the children.

The idea of the Read-Aloud Program developed out of community analysis. In 1987, DPL's marketing department conducted focus groups with African American, Hispanic, and Asian American community leaders to find ways to improve library service. One common request was for the library to "Do more for our children." At that time, the Children's Library manager, Pamela Sandlian, recognized the importance of reading aloud to children. The writings of Jim Trelease helped fuel this belief. Trelease states that, "Every time we read to a child, we're sending a 'pleasure' message to the child's brain. You could even call it a commercial, conditioning the child to associate books and print with pleasure."[2]

Sandlian realized that many young children in the community were not experiencing this pleasure and needed it in order to develop important pre-reading skills. Utilizing a growing collection of beautiful picture books, DPL staff endeavored to design and implement an outreach read-aloud program for preschool children.

In 1988, with a Library Services and Construction Act (LSCA) grant, DPL staff and community volunteers began visiting Head Start classrooms to read stories aloud and give books to the children. These one-time visits were fun for the children but did not build the kind of rapport Sandlian sought. The children were happy to get a free book; but they did not discover how wonderful the library and reading are. Therefore, the following year, the project was increased to a ten-week program with each reader visiting a classroom every week for thirty minutes. The ten-week session allowed children to get to know their readers, listen to 50–60 books, and treasure the gift books at the end of the program.

For the first five years of the Read-Aloud Program funding was tight. The library received LSCA grants, support from the Friends Foundation, and grants from local foundations. When funding was not available, outreach was cut back. Then in 1993 DPL stepped up the commitment to the Read-Aloud Program by creating a permanent position for a Read-Aloud coordinator. Today, the library has a part-time coordinator who trains volunteers, schedules Read-Alouds, and selects and distributes books. The DPL relies upon corporate and foundation grants for the purchase of gift books, some printing costs and other reading support. The outreach is done entirely by community volunteers.

The sixty-plus people who volunteer each quarter are from varied backgrounds. Many of the volunteers are retired or self employed and set aside a morning or afternoon a week to be a reader. Other volunteers are professionals who visit their classrooms over their lunch hours. Still others are college students seeking classroom experience in preparation for teaching positions. If they can read in Spanish as well as English, all the better. As one volunteer, Bill, a spry retiree explained, "This is the 'funniest' job I've ever had. And I get hugs for it." It is true that over the weeks, each reader creates a bond with the children he or she reads to. This connection illustrates to children that the library is a place they can go to find great books and visit library friends.

Children who may never have thought to go to the library come in asking for books and to see their reader. One volunteer stopped by a neighborhood library after her Read-Aloud school visit. A child she read to less than an hour before ran up and hugged her. The girl's father was a bit impatient because his six-year-old daughter, Kathy, insisted on coming to the library immediately after school. Meanwhile, Kathy was searching through books and choosing those she had heard from the library readers. Kathy's enthusiastic response to the books and reading is what brought her and her father to the library. By the end of the visit, the father seemed more interested, too.

The Read-Aloud Program is designed to inspire children to love books and reading. A two-hour training insures that volunteers experience reading and listening in a way that deepens their commitment to the Read-Aloud Program philosophy. Readers are asked to follow well-tested guidelines:

- Begin and end each Read-Aloud session the same way, thereby setting a pattern the children will recognize.
- Focus on the book, reading it all the way through without interrupting, commenting or paraphrasing.
- Introduce each book by stating the title, author and illustrator.
- Hold the book in one place to avoid movements that are distracting.
- Give each word and illustration the attention they need.
- Create ways of drawing the children into stories by using natural voice expression, participation and enthusiasm.
- Treat each child with respect and caring.
- Have fun reading so that the children discover that reading is fun.

The reader presents each book by focusing on the story. The children are not asked questions during the story nor are they required to come to a group consensus about the wolf's merit or the colors of the dragon. The children are given the freedom to experience the book in their individual ways. Jon may be focused on the illustrations. Mia may be softly repeating the words; Shana may be thinking about her Aunt Sally. This traditional approach to reading aloud is relaxing and fun for the children.

The reading style also fosters listening skills and a longer attention span, as one volunteer discovered. Michele Mazzoco, a developmental psychologist and Read-Aloud volunteer, was reluctant to focus on the books rather than her interaction with the children. After she tried the Read-Aloud technique, she was surprised by the children's response. "The children did not lose interest in the stories. Rather, they became better able to sit through the five to seven books I read to them."[3] She discovered how quickly children settle into listening to stories rather than chatting through them.

Children listen and focus on the stories because of the quality of the books. Rebecca, a college student and second year volunteer, said of the children, "They need it so much. They just eat the books up with their eyes." The books selected for this outreach program are chosen carefully. Staff search through shelves of picture books to choose the best of the collection. The titles are age-appropriate, well-written, well-illustrated stories with particular attention to multicultural diversity. They are then combined into "book packs" of five to seven books for a volunteer's weekly session.

Within each pack are one or two concept books, one or two participatory books, a traditional folk tale, a contemporary story and a pop-up or movable part book. For example, Book Pack # 18 consists of:

> *Dinosaurs, Dinosaurs* by Byron Barton (Concept)
> *Five Little Monkeys Jumping on the Bed* by Eileen Christelow (Participatory)
> *Goodnight Moon* by Margaret Wise Brown (Story)
> *Caps for Sale* by Esphyr Slobodkina (Story)
> *Spot's First Walk* by Eric Hill (Lift-the-Flap)
> *Maisy Goes to School* by Lucy Cousins (Pop-Up)

By reading a range of short and long stories, participatory and pop-up books, the children gain a variety of listening experiences within the 30 minute period. The books are chosen for their individual quality and not arranged together by theme. Once a staff reader tried to slip a "theme" reading in and a five-year-old boy rolled his eyes and said, "Oh, no. Not another crocodile book. Don't you have something else?"

The volunteers are encouraged to pick up their weekly book packs early and practice reading them aloud. One six-year veteran of the Read-Aloud Program, Marie, a retired school teacher, describes her Read-Aloud preparation this way: "I pick up my books from the library and take quite a bit of time to practice. I read to two-year-olds and six-year-olds and all the children in between." (She reads to six classrooms a week varying her pacing and intonation with each class.) "I might read the same 'Spot' book to all of them but with a very different expression for each group." This kind of thought and preparation help bring the stories to life. It also insures that children light up when Marie walks in the door. The children's affection for her and excitement about the books is payment far beyond any monetary reward the library could provide.

The tenth and final week of the Read-Aloud session is difficult for both the children and the volunteer readers. Nobody wants to say good-bye, but more classrooms need the service. Some volunteers continue reading to their first class and adopt a new one. Either way, the tenth week is special because each child receives a gift book. The paperback is a copy of a title they have heard from their library reader. A retired media specialist and volunteer said,

> In all my years, I have never been so touched by seeing children and books together as I was when I gave these children their gift books. I explained that a book is a very special thing and needs to be treated with care. They just sat hugging their books. I had to fight back tears, it was so touching.

This gift book, a reminder of the Read-Aloud Program, is given to encourage the children to continue reading at home with their parents.

Reaching parents is another important aspect of the Read-Aloud Program. Parents are invited to join the weekly Read-Alouds at their child's daycare or shelter. The DPL also offers parent meetings in the centers or at the library. The meetings include the same Read-Aloud approach used with children, librarians read great children's books to the parents. If children come to the meeting with their parents, their mom and dad get to see how entranced they are by the stories. The DPL also shares information about library services and encourages parents to share stories as a family. Some parents do not always know the importance of reading to their young children; but they care about their children and are eager to learn ways the library can support them.

Our Read-Aloud Program is requested all over the Denver area. Teachers respond enthusiastically to the service. One teacher explained, "We loved story time (the Read-Aloud) and did the DPL Summer Reading Program at the same time. I think this really helped our children become enthusiastic about reading and the library." Another teacher wrote,

> It was such an exciting and rewarding program. I could see the children's attention spans lengthening each week, and the books were inspiring and

motivating. I believe reading aloud is the single best activity for preschoolers, and this program provided outstanding books.

The Read-Aloud Program also offers another benefit, as one volunteer observed, "This is a good way to expose the teachers as well as the children to good literature."

Some centers are inspired by the Read-Aloud Program. One abuse shelter created a library in the recreation room after DPL provided a reader. Mothers and their children used the library to share quiet times reading together. The children at the shelter so loved reading that one day they formed a human barricade at the door so their library reader could not leave.

It is a mysterious, wonderful thing to see how much a child can be inspired by the books. The Read-Aloud Program techniques seem to touch many children deeply. One volunteer was surprised during her eighth week of reading. She visited a community center that provides day care for children living in homeless and abuse shelters. When she arrived, 25 smiling three-, four- and five-year-old children greeted her as usual. "The Library Lady is here!" exclaimed one. Another wrapped her arms around the reader's knees asking, "Did you bring books to read?" Meanwhile, James, a five-year-old who was usually withdrawn and sat stoically in back, carried a chair to the place she always sat. He moved it with care to the angle she usually chose. Although he still sat in back quietly, his eyes locked onto the books and his face warmed. Later, his teacher told the reader that he had been asking each day, "Is the Library Lady coming today?"

It is difficult to assess the influence the Read-Aloud Program has on each child. Readers notice a progressive increase in attention span and listening ability over the ten weeks. Teachers comment on the children's enthusiasm for books after the program. But, sometimes, a child's response is the best clue to success. One reader happened upon a smiling student in a shopping mall some months after her Read-Aloud visits had ended. The seven-year-old girl excitedly explained to her mother that this was the "Library Lady." Then the girl recited a story word-for-word as the "Library Lady" had read it months before. A similar experience happened with another volunteer. When she went to a first grade class to read for the first time, one girl recognized her. The reader had visited the girl's kindergarten class the previous year. Sabrina, a normally disruptive child in class (due to emotional problems and family upheaval), looked at one of the books and suddenly sat down in front and began reciting the text from memory. It was one of many books she knew by heart.

Not all children memorize the stories, or respond so openly to the readers; yet simple, important things are occurring. Circulation in low-income neighborhoods has increased at the DPL more than 30 percent in the last nine years. Older children (K–2) recognize authors, illustrators, and titles and are more confident when visiting their media center or public library. Younger children are gaining valuable pre-reading and language experiences. As Steve Herb, former president of the Association of Library Services to Children noted: "The foundation for emergent literacy is in preschool experiences with language. And the only sound means of transmitting those experiences is through human interaction, the social aspects of learning."[4] Through the Read-Aloud Program, children experience the social aspects of reading and discover that reading is fun. Read-Aloud volunteers find that, when they finish reading a book, often the only comment is, "Can you read another one?"

Very simply, through the volunteer Read-Aloud Program, DPL has library ambassadors. The volunteers go to where the children are and offer a sample of what can be found in the library. The Read-Aloud Program provides enticing experiences with books and cultivates an enthusiasm for reading and a love of stories. The program is strongly supported by funding from community organizations, foundations and the Friends of the Denver Public Library.

As the Children's Library staff assesses the Read-Aloud Program, they continually discover ways to improve. One way is to build a stronger connection with parents. Ideas for drawing parents and children into the library include family nights at neighborhood libraries, art shows, and reading festivals. Another idea is to leave the book packs with the class for the week between Read-Alouds. This would allow the children more opportunities to interact with the books. One reader tested the idea by leaving a book pack in the center each week. The children began acting out the stories and drawing pictures from the books in their free time. Read-Aloud advocate Jim Trelease points out the benefits of having familiar books available for children. Trelease sites a study in which kindergartners, when given a choice of books to explore on their own, first chose books they had heard, read aloud and knew well.[5]

As DPL explores ways to improve the Read-Aloud Program, the underlying philosophy remains. The readers provide children with wonderful experiences with books and reading. Virginia Mathews, a library advocate confirms this approach:

> Librarians who serve children know a wonderful secret that spurs them on despite budget cuts. They know that every time they share a story, a game, a song with small children, they have a chance to light a flame of perception or leave a memory that will remain forever. It may even make a difference in an entire lifetime.[6]

Through the Read-Aloud Program, the Denver Public Library hopes to "light the flame of perception" and make a difference in the lives of Denver's children.

Notes

1. Barbara N. Kupetz, "A Shared Responsibility: Nurturing Literacy in the Very Young," *School Library Journal* (July 1993): 28–31.

2. Jim Trelease, "Reading Aloud for Reading Readiness," *Journal of Youth Services in Libraries* (Fall 1995): 43–53.

3. Michele Mazzoco, "The Magic of Reading Aloud," *Journal of Youth Services in Libraries* (Spring 1995): 312–314.

4. Steve Herb, "Building Blocks for Literacy: What Current Research Shows," *School Library Journal* (July 1997): 23.

5. Jim Trelease, "Reading Aloud for Reading Readiness," *Journal of Youth Services in Libraries* (Fall 1995): 43–53.

6. Virginia H. Matthews, "Kids Can't Wait...Library Advocacy Now! A President's Paper for Mary R. Somerville, President 1996-97, American Library Association," *School Library Journal* (March 1997): 97–101.

The Beginning with Books–Carnegie Library of Pittsburgh Connection

BY ELIZABETH SEGEL

Beginning with Books is an early intervention literacy program dedicated to increasing significantly the numbers of children who become capable and enthusiastic lifelong readers; in particular, its mission is to close the gap between economically disadvantaged children and their more affluent peers in reading ability and school success. We do this by giving parents and other caregivers whatever help and support they need to provide the early experiences that are the best preparation for learning to read and write.[1] This support for parents and caregivers takes the form of supplying appropriate materials (primarily quality children's books), information, encouragement, and skill building. We also train volunteers to read to children one-on-one in the children's rooms of public libraries. The parents of these children are enrolled in literacy or job training programs. Besides the program for their children, they participate in parent workshops on how to support their children's literacy development.

Beginning with Books was founded in 1984. It did not start out as a library program, but in its third year became an affiliate of the Carnegie Library of Pittsburgh, and this affiliation has proven to be most beneficial to both parties. For the fledgling Beginning with Books, the most important advantage initially was the stature conferred by the library, a stable and highly respected community institution. The library also has donated rent-free space in a branch library and contributed to Beginning with Books salaries. (Currently, the library's contribution makes up approximately

5 percent of the organization's budget; the remaining 95 percent is raised by Beginning with Books in the form of foundation and corporation grants, gifts from individuals, sale of literacy materials developed by Beginning with Books, and fees for services.) Over the years, the affiliation has allowed Beginning with Books to benefit from the expertise of the library's professional staff in areas such as financial management, human resources, graphics, and children's services. At the same time, the Library's director, Robert Croneberger (who died in 1998), gave the co-directors of Beginning with Books his wholehearted support and a considerable degree of autonomy and creativity in developing effective ways of meeting the literacy needs of low income families. Beginning with Books has its own Advisory Board, on which the library's director, deputy director, and head of youth services serve *ex officio*.

An important benefit of the partnership for the Library has been to demonstrate its commitment to reaching a traditionally underserved population, at a time when budgetary constraints have limited the amount of outreach the library could do directly. This demonstrable commitment has very likely been a factor in the county government's increased support of the library in recent years, both in direct appropriations and in support of a regional assets tax of which the Library is a primary beneficiary. Perhaps the most important and basic way that the work of Beginning with Books benefits the Carnegie Library of Pittsburgh and other libraries in our region is its success in bringing into the libraries' orbit families that otherwise might never have come through the doors, since all four Beginning with Books programs have the goal of linking economically disadvantaged families to the public library.

In the early 1980s, Dr. Joan Brest Friedberg and I were teaching children's literature in the English Department of the University of Pittsburgh. Joan, who had worked at one time in the early childhood field, was also working with an excellent local preschool to create a rich literacy environment in the classroom, and I was writing a guide on reading to children with another colleague, Dr. Margaret Mary Kimmel of the University's School of Library of Information Science. Both Joan and I were struck by the persuasive research evidence I was compiling for the book — evidence that reading to children in the preschool years was the most effective way to prepare them to become successful readers and students. This was not widely known at the time, although the publication of Jim Trelease's *Read-Aloud Handbook* (1982),[2] Dr. Kimmel's and my *For Reading Out Loud! A Guide to Sharing Books with Children* (1983),[3] and the report of the National Commission on Reading, *Becoming a Nation of Readers* (1986),[4] followed by First Lady Barbara Bush's eloquent championing of the practice, soon gave the idea widespread currency. A recent comprehensive review of research on reading to preschool children confirms its importance for preventing reading difficulties and for making children's transition from home to school easier.[5]

Our first program, the Gift Book Program, was started with a grant from the Pennsylvania Humanities Council in 1984. We knew that regular home storybook reading tended to be limited to families of middle income or higher, where the practice was passed on from one generation to another as parents wanted to duplicate for their children one of the childhood experiences they remembered most warmly. We also believed that if one had not been read to as a child, one might need a few tips on how to go about this new activity. Finally, we hypothesized that low-income families, few of whom use the public library, might not have at hand the kind of books that successfully engage the interest of a new listener.

So we developed the Beginning with Books Gift Book program. Parents waiting to see the doctor at well-baby clinics of the Allegheny County Health Department in economically depressed neighborhoods were offered a packet of four paperback children's books (*Goodnight Moon, Mother Goose, Peter's Chair,* and *500 Words to Grow On*), plus a pamphlet of tips on reading to children and a flyer with the name, address, and operating hours of the nearest library. A Beginning with Books employee counseled the parents informally about the benefits to young children of listening to stories and gave a few simple tips and warm encouragement. She also suggested that parents supplement the books in the packet by borrowing others from their local library. The resulting 393 pre- and post-distribution questionnaires completed by parents who received the books and the counseling revealed significantly more home storybook reading between parent and child and by the child alone, more purchasing of children's books, and greater appreciation of the books and enjoyment of family sharing, even by parents whose own literacy skills were limited. The question about library use was disappointing, however, in the follow-up questionnaires, completed approximately six months after receipt of the packets. Very few families reported themselves as library users before getting the packets, and the project had virtually no impact on this six months later. To the question: "Do you visit the public library?" more than a few parents answered: "No, we have our own books" or the equivalent. The clear implication was that to use the library was to accept charity. Often the same family had reported owning fewer than ten children's books. We had thought of the major barriers to library use in low-income families as lack of transportation, fear of incurring fines, and feeling intimidated by the library. This was an early example of our learning from the families we serve.

Four years after the pilot Gift Book distribution, a small controlled study of the project was conducted by researchers from the University of Pittsburgh. The study looked at a group of kindergarten children whose parents had received the books and counseling four years previously, and compared them to carefully matched children whose parents visited well-baby clinics at times or places where the project did not operate. Parents reported that the gift books were still being read. More reading to children was going on in these homes than in the control group. The most gratifying finding was that kindergarten teachers rated the children served by Beginning with Books as having significantly higher reading ability and language ability than the control children. Sixty-one percent of the project children were rated in the top third of their class by their teachers in reading ability at the end of kindergarten, as compared to 46 percent of the control group; in language ability, 65 percent of the project children were rated in the top third of the class, versus 42 percent of the control children. Sixty-five percent of the children who had received gift book packets actively participated often in group story time sessions, teachers indicated, as opposed to 33 percent of the control group children.

Another welcome finding was that, although library use had not increased six months after the intervention, when the follow-up questionnaires had been completed, four years later, the families served by the project were visiting the library more often than those who did not receive books and counseling. Perhaps in families that were enabled to begin regular storybook reading, parents were not inclined immediately to use the library (when their children were very young) but eventually were motivated to seek out more books.

The Gift Book Program has changed little in the past 14 years. After the initial disappointing report on its failure to encourage library use, we had decided to include just three books in the packet and to include a coupon "good for another free book" at the nearest library. We supply these books to the libraries in any community where the Gift Book Program operates and orient the librarians to the project's goals, so that they can welcome families who bring the coupons, invite them to sign up for library cards, and help them feel comfortable in the library, knowing that they may be visiting for the first time. Most are delighted to have this means of drawing new patrons; only one reported early in the program that she rarely offered the library card option, since "it's obvious that some of them come only to get their free book."

The Gift Book Program is flourishing. Each year we work with staff of dozens of social service, health, and educational organizations in southwestern Pennsylvania: Head Starts, food pantries, women's shelters, teen parenting programs, health clinics. Kindergartens in economically distressed school districts give the books at the first parent conference of the year and report that attendance has shot up to nearly 100 percent. Staff of the partner agencies choose from the two to three dozen books we recommend, the ones they think will appeal most to the families they serve. We help them tailor the counseling and the conditions of the distribution for maximum impact. In our region, we have reached 7,000 to 8,000 families in each of the past several years with this program. We expect to have increased that number significantly by the end of 1998. This project appeals to corporate underwriters — a restaurant chain, utility companies, a health maintenance organization. We use their contributions to reach needy families in their service area and include an underwriting card in each book packet, identifying the donor.

Beginning with Books has developed training and materials to enable others to replicate or adapt this program. For instance, PPG Industries underwrote Beginning with Books training for representatives of its Public Education Leadership Committee from each plant site and is encouraging employees to undertake a Gift Book distribution with the public school in their communities.

The Gift Book Program can complement the services of the public library, both by helping parents start their children on the road to becoming lifelong readers and by bringing librarians face to face with some of the families they want to serve but would not otherwise see. The program demonstrates vividly the power of the Beginning with Books–Carnegie Library of Pittsburgh partnership, because it probably would not have originated in a library, where books are bought for the loan collection, not for home libraries — where materials are purchased for borrowing by a succession of patrons, not for individual ownership. Yet our experience tells us that children need to have some books of their own, favorite books that can be returned to again and again. Once they have discovered the comfort, knowledge, and delight to be found within a book's covers, they will find their way to the many rich resources of the public library.

In 1987, Beginning with Books started Read Together, the program mentioned above which recruits volunteers to read at libraries to children whose parents are in literacy or job training programs. Sessions are one-on-one and take place weekly or twice weekly. The children range from three to 12 years of age; some remain in the program for years, often with the same volunteer. We currently have more than 140 pairs meeting; volunteers contributed well over 6,000 hours last year. An outside evaluation revealed that the great majority of both parents and volunteers believe that the program boosts the children's reading ability and their reading motivation.

Devora Smith,[6] an adult literacy student, enrolled her son Vance in Read Together when he was two and a half. [We later raised the starting age to three. Two is not too young to be read to, of course, but a two-year-old is too young for a volunteer to manage in a library for an hour, we discovered.] Soon Ms. Smith reported hearing Vance in the darkened bedroom retell for his little sister stories his volunteer had read to him; he also shared with her the picture books he received as gifts from the program. When Vance's sister Crystal was old enough, she too was enrolled in Read Together. Mrs. Smith, who confides that "I never read too well," reports that "I learned a whole lot, too. I be down there [at the library] every Tuesday for Read Together." Now she and the children read back and forth to each other. "Each night we read a chapter book. I read a paragraph, then each of them reads a paragraph."

Devora Smith believes this Beginning with Books program has made a significant difference for her children. "I'm trying to bring them up and introduce them to other things beside the street life. I thank the Read Together program for introducing them to the library. We live at the library. Every time I turn around they want to go to the library. I'll say, 'It's Friday, the library's closed' [meaning their neighborhood branch]. They say, 'We can catch a bus and go to the [main] Oakland library'."

We work most intensively with parents in a Beginning with Books program we call Raising Readers Parent Clubs. These were originally called Read-Aloud Parent Clubs. The name was changed because we learned that some parents were reluctant to enroll because they feared they would have to read aloud in front of a group, evoking bad memories of school round-robin reading sessions. Another reason for the name change is that the goals of the program include introducing home literacy activities besides reading to children and this is better reflected in the new title. The Raising Readers Parent Club program brings parents together for eight weekly workshops. Parents receive a free children's book each week and agree to try to read to their children every day. The first session shares information about the benefits to young children of daily storybook reading and suggestions on how to get started. At subsequent meetings, parents (and grandparents) discuss their children's responses to the books; they problem-solve as a group, and learn more about being responsive to their children's reactions and about choosing appropriate books. In later sessions they learn that certain kinds of talk about books and encouragement of children's attempts at writing maximize the benefits of book-reading.

Clubs have been held for Head Start, Even Start, and Chapter I–Title 1 parents, for adult literacy and job training classes, for teen parenting programs and family support center clients, and for resident councils in public housing communities. Some groups meet at a library; for all others, we include a library visit and tour with every cycle of clubs. We not only conduct these groups ourselves, but increasingly train teachers and others to replicate the program. Several groups have continued meeting on their own after the formal sessions conclude. These groups have been a rich source of valuable staff members for Beginning with Books, several of whom are "graduates" of a Raising Readers Parent Club.

Finally, Project BEACON (the Beginning with Books Early Childhood Outreach Network) sends outreach workers to day care homes and centers in economically depressed neighborhoods where they present an enriched story time for the children and mentor the caregivers. The day care sites receive book collections each year and parents of the day care children receive Beginning with Books Gift Book packets and encouragement to build daily storytimes into their family routine. In addition, children and caregivers can select books to borrow from a minibookmobile driven by the outreach workers. The Story-mobiles, as we call them, also visit many Pittsburgh public housing communities several times a month, where children borrow books for pleasure reading, school reports, classroom sustained silent reading time, and for sharing with siblings, friends, and cousins. This program is similar to outreach done by many libraries and their bookmobiles. In our area, bookmobile service by the library to public housing within the city was ended many years ago when city contributions to the Library's budget were drastically reduced.

Project BEACON differs from some library outreach in that the community outreach workers who implement the program are paraprofessionals. A college degree is not required for the position, and many of the outreach workers are talented, dedicated people whose educational opportunities had been limited by economic constraints. (Beginning with Books supports staff development with a fund that can be drawn upon for course work, seminars, or conferences.) The outreach workers are assisted by AmeriCorps members and by residents of the public housing communities they visit. Another difference between our Story-mobile service and that of the library's bookmobiles is that we do not charge fines for overdue or lost books.

Our work with low-income families has impressed on us how serious a deterrent fines are to library use. Every library borrower incurs a fine sooner or later. When one's income doesn't stretch to cover the month's expenses, a parent usually will decide that the privilege of borrowing books does not justify the risk. We have yet to do a close analysis of lost or damaged books, but it appears that our rate of return is excellent. We make borrowing Story-mobile books contingent on the return of previously borrowed books. With gentle encouragement from the outreach workers, children return home to search for missing books. We supply plastic bags with the Story-mobile logo and Story-mobile staff recommend that children keep their books in the bag when not reading them. The reward for returning books is the privilege of borrowing more books. From a one or two book limit, responsible borrowers work their way up to borrowing five or six books at a time. Children often visit the Story-mobile with friends and try to influence their friends' choices, because they will read their own and then swap books in the two weeks between Story-mobile visits.

One goal of Project BEACON, as of all Beginning with Books services, is to introduce participants to the resources of the library. Day care providers are invited to bring children to the library for special programs, with transportation provided by the project's funders. Story-mobile staff encourage children to visit the nearest library where they will find many more books and other resources than the Story-mobile can carry. The librarian of a branch that serves a largely white population, but which has two predominantly African American public housing communities in its area, believes that increased use of the libraries by families from these communities is due to the Beginning with Books Story-mobile visits there.

She had had difficulty attracting African American patrons but tells us that recently each Saturday several young mothers and their children take the bus to the library from their bleak and isolated public housing community. These regular visitors to the Story-mobile had been encouraged by the Beginning with Books outreach worker to try out the library. The librarian tells us that the mothers select books for the children while the children look at books or enjoy play materials that they don't have at home. (Jigsaw puzzles were a big hit when the families first came.) When the time is near to catch the bus for home, the mothers round up the children and check out their own book selections and the children's. This children's librarian confides that previously, she brought out children's books with African American subject matter only during Black History month. Once these families began patronizing her branch, she created permanent display space for these books. This in turn may make this branch library a more welcoming place for other African American families.

When Beginning with Books does its work well, it creates a hunger for good books and information. One participant in a Raising Readers Parent Club reported at the final session: "This Club has made a profound imprint on my knowledge about quality children's books. I used to think that they were all okay. After all, they had been published. This Club has given me an eye for what is a truly good book for kids." We make sure that the parents and caregivers we work with know that the library is their best source of good books for their children. By linking families to the public library, Beginning with Books has the power to turn a timely but limited intervention into a lifelong literacy-supporting connection.

Notes

1. A. G. Bus, M.H. van-Ijzendoorn, and A.D. Pellegrini, "Joint Book Reading Makes for Success in Learning to Read: A Meta-analysis of Intergenerational Transmission of Literacy," *Review of Educational Research*, 65 (1995): 1–21.
2. Jim Trelease, *The Read-Aloud Handbook* (New York: Penguin, 1982, 1995).
3. Margaret M. Kimmel and Elizabeth Segel, *For Reading Out Loud: A Guide to Sharing Books with Children* (New York: Delacorte, 1983, 1991).
4. R.C. Anderson, E.H. Hiebert, J.A. Scott, and I.A. Wilkinson, *Becoming a Nation of Readers: The Report of the Commission on Reading* (Champaign, Ill.: National Academy of Education, Center for the Study of Reading, 1985).
5. Bus, van-Ijzendoorn, and Pellegrini, "Joint Book Reading."
6. Names have been changed to protect the privacy of families.

For Further Reading

Friedberg, J. B. "Keep Reading My Little Girl." In *Literacy: Interdisciplinary Conversations*, ed. Deborah Keller-Cohen. Cresskill, N.J.: Hampton, 1994.
_____. *Super Storytimes: A Guide for Caregivers*. 1995. Beginning with Books, 7101 Hamilton Ave., Pittsburgh PA 15208-1828.
Needlman, R.; Fried, L. E.; Morley, S.; and Zuckerman, B. "Clinic-Based Intervention to Promote Literacy: A Pilot Study." *American Journal of Diseases of Children* 145 (1991): 881–884.
Segel, E. "'I've Got to Get Him Started Out Right': Promoting Literacy by Beginning with Books." In *Bridges to Literacy: Children, Family, and Schools*, ed. David K. Dickinson. Cambridge, Mass.: Blackwell, 1994.
_____. "Pushing Preschool Literacy: Equal Opportunity or Cultural Imperialism?" *Children's Literature Association Quarterly*, summer 1986: 59–62.
_____. "Side-by-Side Storybook Reading for Every Child: An Impossible Dream?" *The New Advocate* 3 (1990): 131–137.
_____, and Friedberg, J. B. "'Is Today Liberry Day?': Community Support for Family Literacy." *Language Arts* 68 (1991): 654–657.

ACCESS TO
TECHNOLOGY FOR
LOW-INCOME GROUPS

The Free Library of Philadelphia Technology Demonstration Project

BY LILLIAN MARRERO
AND SAM WEINSTEIN

This is a description of a Technology Demonstration Project at the Ramonita G. de Rodríguez Branch of the Free Library of Philadelphia. The project attempts to identify innovative uses of technology and especially those applications of technology used to meet community information needs. The objectives of the project are to provide access to information, learning and literacy through electronic resources and the Internet in low income communities.

Roles and Services of the Free Library of Philadelphia

The Free Library of Philadelphia was incorporated in 1891 upon the initiative of William Pepper who was motivated by a bequest from his uncle, George S. Pepper. The library is organized under two governing boards: the Free Library of Philadelphia Foundation Board of Directors, which oversees private sector funds, and the Free Library of Philadelphia Board of Trustees, which oversees city funds.

The Library's mission is fourfold: to provide educational materials in various formats for learners at all levels; to make available popular materials in a timely manner; to provide accurate and up-to-date reference

80

information using different information technologies; and to develop and enhance preschool programs which will include children, parents and other caregivers.[1]

The library system is composed of 49 branches, three regional libraries, and a central library. The library system also includes the Library for the Blind and Physically Handicapped.

The Free Library of Philadelphia serves Philadelphia's 1.5 million residents, as well as residents of surrounding counties and states. There are 482,513 active cardholders and the library has a circulation of more than 6.5 million books and nonbook materials. In 1997, 4.2 million people visited the library and 379,375 attended public programs.

Two important programs that have attracted children and their parents to the library are: LEAP (Learn, Enjoy and Play), which provides after school homework assistance for hundreds of youngsters throughout the city, and Pre-school Library Learning Centers, which provide unique child-oriented environments for preschoolers, their parents and caregivers.

To build on the successful programs mentioned above and to bring primary updated information that supports the educational needs of the residents of Philadelphia, the Library launched a $50 million fundraising campaign called "Changing Lives" in April 1995. Campaign goals include outreach, collection development, renovation of libraries, endowment and the installation of new information technologies in every branch to connect with the global information network.

The Public Library Role in Technology

The library is aware of the changing roles of public libraries in an age of electronic media. The survey results conducted by the National Commission on Libraries and Information Science (1996) illustrates that public library Internet connectivity is growing at an extremely rapid rate as more libraries embrace electronic information as an essential service to respond to community information needs.[2]

One of the major goals of the Free Library is to increase access of information and encourage technology education and use in the more disadvantaged communities in Philadelphia. The library has initiated different technology projects to reach this goal. It has established an online public access catalog using the DRA Information Gateway software; CD-ROM reference tools are available through network and stand-alone machines in different branches and at the central library; a Free Library of Philadelphia homepage (http://galaxy.einet.net/hytelnet/US800.html), has been developed which provides access to the online catalog, periodicals database, and information about branches and library services. The library also provides links to reference sources on the Internet which respond to community needs. These links are selected by professional librarians.

In 1997, through the Changing Lives Campaign, the library received a major donation from the William Penn Foundation. This grant titled "A Proposal for Model Urban Library Services for Children: A Gateway to the 21st Century" will enable the library to renovate 33 branches and establish state of the art technology and Internet connectivity to meet the formal and informal education and information needs of children and their parents.[3]

The Free Library has always supported the educational goals of all Philadelphians by providing resources that correspond to their diverse needs. Recognizing that technology can be used as a tool to support and enhance learning, on April 5, 1996, the Free Library of Philadelphia opened to the public a computer-training lab at the Ramonita G. de Rodríguez Branch that would serve the needs of a low-income community. It is the only place in the Free Library system where the public can receive computer training in an informal setting. Funded by donations and to a large extent by the Knight Foundation (Knight-Ridder, Inc.), this lab is a demonstration project of skills enhancement using "state-of-the-art" technology as well as special programming designed to promote intergenerational learning and use of the library as a community center for information and learning.[4]

Enhancing this Technology Demonstration Project is the Free Library's participation in the Bridge Project. This is a collaborative project between the Free Library of Philadelphia, LibertyNet, Comcast, the Mayor's Office of Community Services, WHYY, Inc., and several other nonprofit organizations. It is funded by the National Telecommunications and Information Administration, an agency of the U.S. Department of Commerce. Concentrating on the Philadelphia Empowerment Zone, this project is designed to make available to the Zone residents Internet access, e-mail accounts and training in Internet use. In the spring of 1994, the Federal government designated three Empowerment Zone areas in Philadelphia to create jobs, build new housing, provide job training and establish health and human services programs. The Bridge Project offers a model for using computer technology to support economic and community development in low-income communities.[5]

Description of the Community

The Ramonita G. de Rodríguez Branch is located one mile north of center-city Philadelphia and the Liberty Bell. It serves a community of 21,984 residents of whom 5,643 are White, 15,494 are African American and 4,269 are of Hispanic origin. The median family income is $22,459, with 35 percent living below the poverty level. Seventeen percent of the residents are unemployed. There are 7,847 households in this area and single women head 2,628 of them. Of a total of 15,769 adults 18 years or older, 5,316 did not graduate from high school and only 2,101 have taken any college courses. After English, Spanish is the predominant language spoken in the community.[6]

The Rodríguez branch serves the American Street Empowerment Zone. This area has its own particular demographic characteristics. According to the 1990 census, there were 15,486 area residents, of which 61 percent are Hispanic, 20 percent are white and 18 percent are African American. Zone residents live in 4,639 households and single women head 36 percent of the households. Children from birth through age 18 make up 37 percent of the residents; adults 19 through 44 make up 39 percent of the residents. Over 20 percent of the residents are unemployed and 53 percent have incomes below the poverty level. Among residents age 18 and over, 28 percent have graduated from high school and 30 percent of the adult residents have less than a ninth grade education and 33 percent left school between the ninth and twelfth.[7]

Project Goals

In order to meet the social, informational, and academic needs of the adults and children successfully, the Technology Demonstration Project and the Bridge Project were blended into the Rodríguez Branch Computer Training Lab. The Technology Demonstration Project has the following goals:

- To increase family and community use of the library as a learning and information center where children, teenagers, parents, grandparents and caregivers can explore books, videos, cassette tapes and computer programs.
- To create a model program which will enable the library to customize programs for increasing the usage and effectiveness of the electronic library in communities at risk.
- To provide direct assistance and training in the use of computers and other information technologies through individual assistance, training sessions, workshops and other programming events.
- To enhance success in school and the workplace through technology-assisted learning and skill building.
- To create a base of library users who are trained and comfortable with computers as a tool for information access.
- To forge links between community-based educational programs and

the library's (technological) resources in order to enhance and reinforce educational programming of local agencies.

The Bridge Project goals are:

- To reinforce and enhance the learning of low-income residents and to develop their skills using these new technologies.
- To introduce them to opportunities to participate in community life using telecommunications technologies.
- To connect them with job and business information.

Description of the Project and Activities

The Computer Training Lab is staffed with two part-time computer trainers, a full-time bilingual librarian and the project manager. The coordinator of the Bridge Project is LibertyNet, a local Internet service provider dedicated to meeting the on-line needs of the nonprofit community. They offer technical support and overall coordination, host Web pages for the various project members and offer space for e-mail accounts on their mail server. The Rodríguez Computer Lab contains five networked multimedia PCs with Internet access and one projector. On the adult side of the main floor of the Ramonita G. de Rodríguez branch there are four additional networked multimedia PCs and three more on the children's side. Patrons take the workshops at the Lab and practice what they have learned using the library's computers. The Lab as well as the branch is open six days a week most of the year. The Lab and the branch are each open approximately 44 hours a week.

To meet the goals of the projects the Computer Lab created three main programs: The Computer Training Program, which emphasizes training on computer use, office applications and "edutainment" software; the Information Technology Program (the Bridge Project), which emphasizes training on the use of the Internet, on-line databases, and the design and creation of web pages; and the Literacy Program, which emphasizes the use of interactive ESL and GED software to achieve academic and educational goals.

The Computer Training Program

Computer literacy has become an indispensable skill in our society. A great percentage of the adult residents that live near the Rodríguez branch hold low-paying jobs due to their low educational achievement as well as lack of employable skills such as computer literacy. Many of them lack the financial resources to buy a computer for home use. On the other hand, many families do not, because of work or financial constraints, have the time or money to enrich their children's experiences beyond the classroom. Yet children can benefit from using computers to improve their critical thinking skills as well as reading and writing skills. To respond to these needs the Computer Lab developed a series of programs for adults and children.

Adult Technology Workshops

One of the goals of the computer training workshops is to develop computer literacy skills in the adult population in order to improve their potential employability. Workshops include the following topics: An Introduction to Windows 95, Beginning Word for Windows, Intermediate Word for Windows, Excel, PowerPoint, Access, Desktop Publishing, Resume Writing, and Typing. Workshops range from one and one-half to three hours in length and people can repeat them at any time. Seventy percent of the adults that first participated in the program did not have any previous experience with computers and came with "technology phobia" thinking that they would not be able to master the computer.

At the end of the first workshop most of the trainees experience a sense of empowerment when they felt that they were in control and able to go through the tasks and exercises that the training required. Ninety percent of them continued to take up to five different workshops and some of them obtained a computer certification that the program provides. Since we have a sizable Spanish speaking population, we do offer several workshops such as PC Basics, Beginning Word for Windows and the Internet in Spanish. Handouts for these workshops are available in Spanish as well as English. The part-time computer trainer is bilingual, as is the full-time librarian.

Children's Technology Workshops

The U.S. Department of Education promotes the use of technology in schools, libraries, and communities to achieve its mission of ensuring equal access to education and promoting educational excellence throughout the nation.[8]

The Department of Education generates technology initiatives in the belief that the success of the nation will depend substantially on students' ability to acquire the skills and knowledge necessary for high-technology work and informed citizenship. Properly used, technology increases students' learning opportunities, motivation, and achievement and helps students to acquire skills that are rapidly becoming essential in the workplace.[9]

In low-income communities, public libraries have become learning centers for students who need to access information and acquire the educational skills that will help them stay in school. At the Free Library of Philadelphia two programs fill those needs. The Bits and Bytes program trains students in using the World Wide Web and helps them get the educational information they need to complete their school tasks. LEAP, the after-school homework help program helps students to do their homework. Through both of these programs the library has played a major role in influencing students' attitudes toward learning, self-confidence, and self-esteem.

In addition to these programs, the Computer Lab holds training sessions for parents and children every week. The training consists of showing them how to use the "edutainment" software that is available through the library computers. These software programs combine educational and entertainment activities designed to instruct while children play. Some parents come with the children to learn together the use of the software and some children come by themselves because they are self-motivated. The software programs are geared to develop reading, writing, math and language skills as well as critical thinking. Programs such as Math Blaster, the Reader Rabbit series, the Berenstain Bears series, the Living Books series and Kid Pix are used for the younger children.

Older children learn to use the Encarta encyclopedia and the Student Writing Center, which is a word processing program to write their school reports. Children are also encouraged to develop their typing skills by using Kid's Typing.

Library Partnerships with Schools

Since many local schools do not have Internet access yet, the Rodríguez Library and particularly the Computer Lab have established working relationships with the schools as well as after-school programs in the area. The goal is to provide Internet training to teachers and students and to promote the different services that the library provides for children and parents.

Information Technology Program
(The Bridge Project)

Computer ownership and use of the Internet have grown at a faster rate every year. In July 1995, there was approximately seven million Internet hosts worldwide compared to one million hosts in July of 1992.[10] However, there is a great disparity in the accessibility of technology based on socioeconomic status (Lewis, 1996). Nationally, 39 percent of households have computers; in Philadelphia, only 15 percent of households have access to them. The two most significant factors determining access to computers are education and income. How important is it to provide access to technology, and how can these new tools improve the lives of the city's economically and educationally disadvantaged communities? Lewis stated in her article that we "first must establish that technology access is, in and of itself, knowledge," that by simply "surfing the web or exchanging electronic mail with another person is, in itself, teaching the user new skills." The Federal Government has developed a series of initiatives that support this concept. For example, the KickStart initiative establishes that the "Information Superhighway will affect and improve the lives of individuals of all ages, as well as the nation's educational system, business environment, and the very fabric of community life."[11]

The Bridge Project is a collaborative effort with LibertyNet, different nonprofit organizations, and the Free Library. Through the project, a network of three community computing centers was created in the three Empowerment Zone (EZ) neighborhoods in the city. The Rodríguez Computer Lab is the center providing service to the residents that live in the American Street Empowerment Zone.

Through an array of workshops and educational activities, the project looks to create and support the access of low-income residents to information that can provide small business development and individual self-sufficiency. It also intends to reinforce and enhance the learning of low-income residents, develop their skills using telecommunication technologies, introduce them to opportunities to participate in community life using telecommunication technologies and connect them with job and business information. Training programs designed to target special needs include Practical Uses of the Internet, Internet for Educators, Fundraising on the Internet and Job-Hunting on the Internet.

In their role as information providers, trainers also introduce the Free Library on-line catalog as well as different databases available through the library's website. Trainees learn, for example, how to search for a library resource using different Boolean search strategies. They learn about the special events and programs hosted by different branches around the city. They also visit some of the links recommended by the library staff, such as the City of Philadelphia Civil Service Job Opportunity website and Philadelphia government agencies. Information is given on how to apply for a city job and where to turn for particular services provided by the city.

The project also encourages on-line communication between community residents and the nonprofit organizations serving the area as well as other Empowerment Zones throughout the country. To achieve this objective, Empowerment Zone residents and nonprofit organizations are eligible for free e-mail accounts. The e-mail component of this program uses Netscape Mail. LibertyNet provides dummy training accounts for those who have not yet applied for their personal account.

Nonprofit organizations in the Empowerment Zone will benefit from the project by creating a website and by providing services on-line which support the needs of the Empowerment Zone residents.

The Internet Mentoring Program for Teens

One major goal of the Bridge Project is to help nonprofit organizations provide services on-line. This requires developing and maintaining a website. Since staff members of nonprofit organizations do not have the time to develop a website, the project created the Internet Mentoring Program for Teens. This program matches community teens with community organizations. The teens volunteer their time to help the organization with the HTML coding and the graphics. In return for their time and volunteer efforts, the teens learn a valuable skill and also create a personal website hosted by LibertyNet.

The program began in the fall of 1996. Ten teens participated in the initial program and helped to create web pages for five organizations. Since the program was so successful, the Rodríguez Computer Lab organized a second group of volunteers as a summer program.

Literacy Program

A key component of this project is adult literacy. The area served by the Rodríguez Library is marked by a low high school graduation rate. Many residents are of Hispanic origin and speak very little English or none at all. Software was purchased for the GED and ESL components of the technology demonstration project and has been integrated into existing GED and ESL classes. Community College of Philadelphia uses the software for its GED and ESL classes and the Center for Literacy also uses the GED software. The software that is used for the GED class is Contemporary GED Interactive and for the ESL class it is English Discoveries and Rosetta Stone. Since most of the learners have no computer experience, the programs were chosen based on the following criteria: they are easy to use, they require minimal instruction, they monitor student progress, and they are highly interactive.

Conclusion

More than 3,800 people have participated in Computer Training Lab activities during the period from April 1996 through May 1997. Both projects will be evaluated based on different criteria by outside evaluators. In addition the Lab maintains a database of people who have been trained in different workshops and have participated in different educational activities. Formative evaluation is conducted by using evaluation forms at the end of each training session. In response to the evaluations, changes were made in the content of workshops and activities that respond better to the participant's needs. For example, workshops such as Typing, PowerPoint, Intermediate Word for Windows and Access were added; training manuals were translated in Spanish and each workshop was made longer with additional exercises to practice and reinforce the learning experience.

While it is relatively easy to quantify computer and library use, measuring the human impact of such services and training remains a daunting task. We see many new users coming to the library; many of them are eager to make use of the workshops and their new library card. By any measurement, our project must be considered a success.

More always needs to be done. For example, we need to find ways to attract more people to the GED and ESL pieces of the Lab and to motivate them to improve their situation. On the other hand, we do not know to what extent the individuals who went through the technology training are using the World Wide Web. Nevertheless, we do know that the acquisition of these new skills and the information acquired through the training will empower them as well as the community where they live.

Notes

1. E. J. Rodger and G. D'Elia. *When They Turn to Us: Serving Diversity: The Free Library of Philadelphia Long-Range Service Plan 1991–1996.* Philadelphia: Free Library, 1990.
2. National Commission on Libraries and Information Science Reply Comments (1996). URL: http://www.nclis.gov/info/fcc2.htm

3. The Free Library of Philadelphia Foundation. *A Proposal for Model Urban Library Services for Children: A Gateway to the 21st Century.* Philadelphia: Free Library, 1996.

4. The Free Library of Philadelphia Foundation. *The Two Year Technology Demonstration Project.* Philadelphia: Free Library, 1995.

5. LibertyNet. *The Bridge Project: A Collaborative Model for Empowering Low-Income Communities.* Philadelphia, University City Science Center: LibertyNet, 1995.

6. D. Root. *Community Profile Ramonita G. de Rodríguez Branch.* Philadelphia: Free Library, 1996.

7. Philadelphia Empowerment Zone [American Street Neighborhood Profile]. Unpublished raw data, 1994.

8. U.S. Department of Education (1997, June 16). *Technology Initiatives.* URL: http://www.ed.gov/Technology/

9. U.S. Department of Education (1996, June 29). *Getting America's Students Ready for the 21st Century: Meeting the Technology Literacy Challenge.* URL: http://www.ed.gov/Technology/Plan/

10. Lewis, P. F. (1996). *Universal Access to the Internet: Can We Narrow the Knowledge Gap?* URL: http://grove.ufl.edu/%7Epflewis/mmc6402.html#Top

11. National Information Infrastructure Advisory Council (NIIAC) (1996). *The KickStart Initiative.* URL: http://www.benton.org/Library/KickStart/kick.home.html

Neighborhood Coalition and International Organization

Libraries in the Street

BY DENIS CRETINON AND CARL EGNER

The American Library Association promotes equal access to
information for all persons, and recognizes the urgent need to
respond to the increasing number of poor children, adults, and
families in America. These people are affected by a combination
of limitations, including illiteracy, illness, social isolation,
homelessness, hunger, and discrimination, which hamper the
effectiveness of traditional library services. There it is crucial that
libraries recognize their role in enabling poor people to participate fully in a democratic society, by utilizing a wide variety of
available resources and strategies.[1]
> — The American Library Association Policy Manual

The children in the neighborhood were not going to the public
library so the Fourth World volunteers brought a library to them.
The children feel that the street library is their library, where they
can make new friends and learn about children from different
countries and different cultures. They learn, too, that children are
the same wherever they come from. The street library encourages
the children to study more. They can read books, they choose and
even learn with a computer. The children become more interested
in reading, and reading skills are essential for the children to succeed in school. The street library supports the children and their
parents in the children's efforts to do better in school.
> — Maria Clores, a mother from New York City

Some may question whether it is appropriate for men and women
to go into very poor areas with only a few books or paintbrushes
and crayons in their bags, when there are families who have no
home, no work and very little to eat. Yet people welcome them in
their communities and homes; they understand that these men
and women come to share, not their surplus; but who they are,

they feel recognized in their aspirations for dignity, artistic
creation and new relationships.[7]
— Joseph Wresinski, founder of the Fourth World Movement

The American public library system is a clear manifestation of the basic American belief that knowledge should be available to all, black or white, rich or poor, educated or illiterate. As with other resources, however, libraries tend to be used more by people who already have more means. For many, if not most, families living in persistent poverty, libraries remain foreign territory. The American Library Association has recognized this, and has written a clear set of guidelines on how to make libraries more accessible to the poor, and there are certainly many outstanding efforts being made toward this end in libraries across the country.

The authors of this article, however, believe that community-based programs which put a premium on identifying, reaching, and working with the poorest members of a community and which are staffed by caring and committed people — like the street library program of the Fourth World Movement — also have a vital role to play in creating links between the very poor and community institutions like public libraries. The stories about the street libraries in this article are true but the names of the participants have been changed.

Katia

Katia lives in the East New York section of Brooklyn. She and her family live on a block plagued by drug dealing and violence. We always made a special effort to invite Katia to the street library but it was not easy at first for her to participate. She was very shy, and was teased by the other children because she was quite behind for her age.

Katia's mother was very supportive of the street library and encouraged her daughter to come. She said to us, "Before, I lived in a welfare hotel, and Katia went to an after-school program. But she never learned how to read. Her brother tries to help her but it is not enough. But with the street library, they come every week, and now, Katia loves books and reading."

One day we had brought a computer to the street library. Children were using it to write short texts, as part of an ongoing project we were doing. Several children wanted to use the computer at the same time, so we had to intervene, to make a list so the children would go one by one. Katia wanted to use the computer too, but two boys said that she should not be given the chance because she could not recognize the letters on the keyboard. Katia was eight or nine at the time, and it was true that she had a hard time recognizing the letters.

I refused to listen to the two boys and instead let Katia use the computer first. She said what she wanted to write, and the volunteers spelled the words for her. It took her a long time to find the letters. The boys who were waiting wanted to help her or to type on the keyboard for her. But we insisted that the others would only show the keys to her, and she typed them in by herself.

Katia was so proud when out of the printer came the words she had typed, "I love my mother. Katia." She went immediately up to her apartment to bring the paper home, and a couple of weeks later the paper was still hanging on the wall in the living room.

Another time we were reading books on the sidewalk and sitting on blankets. The weather was nice. Katia was there, but it was never easy to read books with her. She did not know how to read and some other children were making fun of her. She would sit next to me and try to guess a word or a letter, and I would correct her word by word. Often children who have a hard time prefer to try each word and be corrected for each one rather than being read to because it shows that they know how to read. Katia was like this as well.

After a time, however, I got her to listen while I read a book to her. I read a wonderful book called *Leo the Late Bloomer*.[3] It is about a baby tiger named Leo who does not know how to do anything: He cannot read, write, draw, or eat neatly. His father worries a lot about him, but Leo's mother counsels patience. Nothing changes during a whole winter and summer. But then, suddenly, in his own good time, Leo blooms and learns how to do everything. He even learns how to talk and says, "I can do it!"

Katia loved the story. Her eyes didn't leave the book. She asked me to read it several times. It was like a magic time. Then the street library continued and we left a while later.

When we came back the next week, we were just starting to spread the blankets on the sidewalk and to open the bookcase. We had not yet gone to call the children, but Katia was there already. She wanted to read *Leo the Late Bloomer*. It was still in the bookcase and we sat down to read it. "I'll read to you," said Katia. I was surprised, but let her take the book. She opened it right up and began. "Leo did not know how to do anything," said Katia, and she turned the page. "He did not know how to read." Page after page, Katia told the whole story, almost exactly as it was printed in the book. Katia had not learned how to read in a week, but to my big surprise she had remembered the whole story since the previous week! Katia was so proud and happy.

That was several years ago. Earlier this year, Katia's mother explained that her daughter was now doing much better in school. Today Katia is 14. She continues to do well in school. Last month she talked to me about e-mail, the Internet and how she would like to have a pen pal in another country.

Often, when we ask families about what the street library means to them, they tell us that we taught their children how to read and write. But we never do this. Through the street library, as Katia's mother says, children discover books in a new light. Books become fun, like games. Putting a book in front of a child does not make him or her learn how to read, but if children discover that books can be relevant to their own lives, can make them proud of themselves, their families, their buildings and neighborhoods, then children can feel a motivation to learn to read. That's why books such as *Leo the Late Bloomer* are so important.

One Thursday Afternoon: A Typical Street Library

Today is street library day. At about the time school ends, two Fourth World volunteers pull their van in front of the apartment building. "You're late today," says Sherelle. "I have been waiting for you."

There is some sun today. Many people are outside on the street. Some women sit on the stoop. Two men are chatting in their car a little further. There are children playing and laughing and running as usual. Soon, however, some children are also reading books on blankets laid out on the sidewalk. There is also a long extension cord coming out of a first floor apartment window, the apartment of Mr. and Mrs. Agee. The cord leads to a computer set up on a little wall in its yellow wooden box. A child is sitting on a milk crate in front of the computer.

We go around to knock at the door of each family on the block which has children from about six to 12 years old. "Today is the street library. Does Tiffany want to come?" "Tiffany is going to come in a minute. I am dressing her up. What are you going to do today? Did you bring the computer?"

Sometimes the doors stay closed, other times we receive a polite negative answer. We will continue, however, to knock at each door. It can take time for the families to trust us enough to send their children outside with us. Ms. Agee, who first invited us to come to this block, has also introduced us to many of her neighbors, and this is crucial in helping us gain, little by little, the confidence of the other families.

On the blanket on the sidewalk, we open up our book case—a big book-shaped wooden box that we made with children in Harlem two years ago—and welcome the children who arrive. Depending on the season and what we have planned for each day, we can see anywhere from three to forty children! We prepare the street library for the six to 12 year olds, but very often children come with their baby brothers or sisters. We always have a couple of small board books for them.

Tiffany arrives. She wants to read me a book. I help her with the words she doesn't know. Children are sitting alone or in groups of two or three. I make a deal with Michael. He reads one page; I read the other one. This way it will not take too long to finish the book. With three other children we read and play with the book about the woman who ate a fly. The children laugh out loud. We read the story three times.

Some older boys are passing by with their bicycles. They look at us but do not stop. One of them, Peter, does not know how to read. He sometimes is a bit provocative with us, teasing us or telling us that what we do is corny. I open a game book in front of them. It contains beautiful pictures in which the children have to find different objects. Today we succeed in making the boys stop to join us. They like this game book. We play together with the book for about fifteen minutes. Maybe next time they will stop for a story or look at a documentary book with us.

Some parents are also nearby, looking at us from their windows or sitting near us on the stoop. A father has brought his two year old boy, put him down on the blanket, picked up a book and put it his hands: "Read, Jason, read!" Some parents take the time to read a book with their children.

While we are reading, not everyone stays still. Some of the more energetic kids come and go. They switch between reading and playing basketball at a homemade hoop on the electric pole. They have to stop their game with each passing car.

The reading time usually ends with one of the volunteers reading a story out loud. Today we are going to act out a story, "The Stone Soup." We set up the street stage, two wooden posts standing on a base, with a nice black fabric stretched between them. The audience sits on a blanket. There are a few props, and simple costumes. The audience is good and they participate in the play. They sometimes jump up to the stage or go behind the stage, but one mother is there to help us keep order. She likes the story, with its repeated catch phrase, "Fancy that, soup from a stone!" Three months later, she still laughs when she repeats it to me.

The play is finished. Some voices in the audience ask, "What are we going to do today?" It seems we have done a lot already, but the children are anxiously awaiting the activity time. Over the past few weeks, we have been making beautiful greeting cards that we send to children who participate in street libraries in Switzerland, Belgium, and France. We have now received some answers, but the cards are written in foreign languages. The children cannot understand the cards at all, so we decide to make a little skit. We have a cardboard mailbox, a model plane and a globe. We show the children how their cards traveled to these other countries, and we play a tape we prepared beforehand with a few sentences in each of the different languages. At each stop of the plane we play the tape to let them hear French, German, and Dutch. The children are puzzled. "I don't understand anything." "What's that? It's not Spanish!" The kids ask us to speak a bit more. We say some more words and phrases in these languages and they laugh.

Our theme at the street libraries over the last months has been "communication." Next week we will tell them about two children who had been friends but then one moved to a different city. What means can the two friends use to communicate? For each idea we will put a string between two cardboard characters we prepared.

Next week we will make a simple electric telegraph machine and communicate in Morse Code between the two sides of the sidewalk.

For this day, however, the street library is over. It is after five o'clock. Some children have already left. Two or three stay and help us fold the blankets, put the books in the bookcase and roll it on its wheels to the van. Sherelle sneaks inside the van while we were not looking and we have to make her come out. "When are you coming back?" she asks. But she knows the answer already. As her parents told us, "Sherelle looks forward to the street library. Several times during the week she asks us, 'Is it Thursday yet, is it time for the street library?'"

Mark and Richie

Mark and Richie O'Neil are from Coney Island, in New York City. They were always among the most faithful participants in the Coney Island street library. They were usually right there to greet us when we drove up in our van, and almost always were still there when we pulled away after the activity was over. They did not, however, participate very much in the actual street library activities. They were always there, hovering around the fringes of the street library, but it was a major challenge to get them to sit down quietly for even a few minutes.

Mark and Richie are brothers, although that is not immediately obvious at first glance. Mark is big and husky, Richie thin and wiry. They live on the sixth floor of a 14-story public housing project. Another building of the same size is located right next to it. These buildings are only three blocks from the Coney Island beach, but they are almost completely cut off from the normal life of the city. Mark and Richie's family, like almost all the families in the those two buildings, is very poor.

We had been holding street libraries in Mark and Richie's neighborhood for several years, and we had gotten to know both of them and their family quite well. Mark and Richie were hard to miss at the street library. They were constantly running around, often in a very disruptive way, and the other children were constantly taunting them. The other children would say, "Don't bother with Mark and Richie; they're no good anyway." For all these reasons, Mark and Richie became the objects of special attention from us. If we could make the street library work for them, it would work for all the children. Eventually, not only did they become important members of the street libraries, they also led us to the public library in Coney Island.

The street library always has the goal to move beyond itself and to make links between the families who participate in the street libraries and the larger community. In Coney Island, we wanted to try to link up with the local public library. The library that serves the area where the O'Neil family lives is about twenty blocks away. There are public buses that go between the buildings of the projects and the library — situated in "downtown" Coney Island — but most families could not afford to pay a bus fare for trips to libraries, even if they had been motivated to go.

We also thought that the library might be a place to meet with the children of the street libraries when the weather made it impossible to be outside. We went to visit the library and spoke with the librarians. We spoke of our concern that the children we knew and worked with through the street libraries were not really taking advantage of the facilities offered by the library. The librarians responded that they knew that there were parts of the Coney Island community which did not use the library, and they wanted to reach out, but did not know how.

We knew that for most of the families in the projects the library was like another world; they just never went there. We did not know how the families would react toward going to the library, but felt that everyone had something to gain from such a project.

Our next step was to go to visit the families in the projects, to ask their opinion about going to the library. Most of the parents were enthusiastic, but not all the children wanted to go. It was thanks to Richie and his family that we finally understood why.

When we went to visit the O'Neils to ask about the idea of taking the children to the library, Mrs. O'Neil thought it was a wonderful idea. Richie, however, had a different opinion. Everyone could see that he was not happy about the idea, but he would not say why. All he would say was, "Stupid library!" He was clearly upset.

When we left that day we did not know why Richie was upset, but later, with the help of Mrs. O'Neil, we did discover why. Richie had actually been to the public library, with his school class. All the children in the class had been encouraged to borrow books, five for each child. Each child was also issued his or her own library card. Richie was at first happy to have the books, but he was never able to return them. First of all the library was far away for him, and by the time the books were due to be returned, Richie had forgotten about them. Eventually he started to get notices from the library about overdue books, but by that time he could not even find the books. Probably one or more of the many people who pass through the O'Neil apartment had picked up the books. Richie continued to get notices from the library, and they said he would have to pay what for him seemed like enormous fines. Richie ended up being terrified of going back to the library.

We saw we were confronted with a serious obstacle to going to the library with the children, and soon discovered that other children from the projects had had similar experiences. We decided to go to see the librarians, and explained to them the situation of most of the families we knew in the projects, for whom it was very difficult to borrow books from a library and have them ready to be returned in good conditions three weeks later. Most of the families had almost no books of their own in their homes, and most apartments were seriously overcrowded. The combination of all these circumstances made it almost inevitable that library books would get lost or damaged.

The librarians were enthusiastic about the idea of bringing children from the projects to the library, and they were even eventually willing to forgive the outstanding fines owed by many of the children. We requested that the librarians not push at first the idea that the children could get library cards and borrow books. We felt that the children should first have the chance to get comfortable with the library, and that the library had plenty to offer the children beyond just borrowing books. Only later we started to help the children get library cards, guaranteeing to the library that we would help the children to bring the books back.

Throughout a whole school year, we went each week to the library with a small group of children. Most street library sessions at the projects were attended by twenty to thirty children, and the children were completely free to come and go as they pleased. The atmosphere was lively, noisy, full of laughter and shouting. A library, obviously, has a completely different atmosphere. We had to take much smaller groups of children, only six to eight children with two or three adults. We also were able to build a different kind of relation with the children; we could work much more personally with certain children.

The librarians were extremely helpful. They very much wanted to make this experiment work. They provided our group a special space for ourselves where we could experiment with a computer. The librarians regularly read stories to the children. They helped the children find materials they needed for their schoolwork. And the next summer, some of the librarians even agreed to come to visit some street library sessions in the project. This latter step was very important in gaining the confidence of the families living in the projects. The librarians demonstrated in a very concrete way their desire to go out and meet the families on their own territory.

After our project with the Coney Island library was over, Mark Levine, the branch librarian, wrote the following letter to Bruno Tardieu, the Fourth World Volunteer who was the leader of the street libraries at that time:

> For several years now members of the Tapori Street Library have been working closely with the Coney Island branch of the Brooklyn Public Library in an effort to reach out to a segment of the Coney Island community that might otherwise be overlooked. During the school year the Tapori group brings children to the library on a regular basis. During the visits the librarians, along with the Tapori members, help the children select books that are of interest to them or that may help them with school assignments. In addition the librarians and Tapori members tell the children stories.
>
> During the summer months the Tapori Street Library provides weekly storytelling and other children's activities directly in the Coney Island community. The librarians from the Coney Island branch assist the Tapori group with these programs.
>
> Many of the children that Tapori brings to our library have no other means of coming here; most have not seen the inside of any library before coming here. The public library's traditional role is to serve all members of the community, rich or poor and young and old, in their pursuit of learning and knowledge. Tapori should be commended in helping the library reach out to some of the less fortunate children in our community.

Tapori is the name of the children's branch of the Fourth World Movement, and the street libraries in New York at that time were called Tapori Street Libraries. This project was an opportunity for the community of Coney Island. The librarians learned more about the reality of some of the poorest residents of the area. The families learned that the library really wanted to make them welcome. And many of the children saw that the library could become a real resource for them. They learned how to take advantage of it.

For Richie and Mark this project was especially important. The sessions in the public library allowed us to give a kind of special attention to the O'Neil boys that was not often possible in the street libraries. This led to building the kind of confidence which is so necessary in helping the poorest people break out of their isolation.

Origins of the Fourth World Movement

The Fourth World Movement was founded in France in 1957, when a French parish priest, Joseph Wresinski, was sent to be the chaplain for an emergency housing camp in the town of Noisy-le-Grand, on the outskirts of Paris. In Noisy, over 250 families were living in metal Quonset huts, with no running water, no electricity and no paved streets. This shantytown had such a bad reputation that the local post office refused to deliver mail to the individual dwellings. Mail was dropped off for all the families at an office at the entrance to the camp.

Father Joseph had himself grown up in severe poverty, so he immediately identified the families in that housing as his own people, and he dedicated the rest of his life to working with such families to end once and for all the plague of persistent human poverty. He and the families living in the camp founded a self-help organization which eventually grew into the Fourth World Movement. The Fourth World Movement today has projects in about 25 countries, in Europe, North America, South America, Asia, and Africa, and corresponds with people in some one hundred countries.

From the first days of his life in this camp, Father Joseph realized that these families were so poor and so isolated that they would not alone be able to break the vicious circle of their situation. From the beginning of his time there Father Joseph invited others to come to work with him. Many people came to help, but a small number of people also decided to stay on with Father Joseph and to make a long-term commitment to living and working alongside the very poor. Father Joseph called these people "volunteers," and today the Fourth World Volunteer Corps founded by Father Joseph has about 350 members. They are married and single, practice many faiths or philosophies, and come from all walks of life. They often live and work in close partnership with very poor families, and all of them accept a small living allowance as their only salary.

Father Joseph also worked from the very beginning to inform the rest of the society about what he was doing. He wrote articles, newsletters, and books; founded a research institute on extreme poverty; and generally set out to engage people of all walks of life in this effort to overcome persistent poverty.

The Fourth World Movement today runs literacy training, skills training, health programs, street libraries, cultural projects, and people's universities with very poor families all over the world. It is active in working with and representing the very poor at local, national, and international levels. All these efforts are based on a core set of beliefs which can be summarized in the following points:

- all human beings have an innate dignity that can never be taken away or destroyed, whatever the conditions of one's life;
- projects with the very poor should include an important element of acquiring and sharing knowledge about the lives of the very poor;
- projects should be based on the expectations and aspirations of the poorest people;
- projects should work towards building partnerships between the very poor and the rest of the community;
- projects must be developed with the specific goal in mind of reaching the very poorest members of the community;
- and, in order for the condition of the very poor to truly change, society as a whole must accept the very poor as full partners in the development of the society.

The Fourth World Movement in the United States

The first Fourth World volunteers in the United States came from Europe in the early sixties. At about that time, Father Joseph had heard about the American war on poverty, and he was convinced that it was an enormous opportunity for the very poor all over the world. He felt that the Fourth World Movement needed to learn from the American war on poverty, and vice versa.

In those early years, the Fourth World Volunteers lived and worked in the Lower East Side of Manhattan. The Lower East Side had always been a neighborhood where immigrant groups settled in New York, and still in the 1960s nearly everyone in the neighborhood was poor. For the next fifteen years, the Fourth World Movement was a constant presence in the neighborhood. They ran a variety of programs — preschools, a drop-in center for teenagers, meetings for adults — all of which were designed to reach the most vulnerable families in the area.

During this same period, however, the neighborhood itself was changing dramatically. In the mid seventies, the long but relentless process of
gentrification started to be felt by most of the families known to the Fourth
World volunteers. Fires in the tenement buildings became commonplace,
and more and more families were forced to move out of their apartments.
Many families from the Lower East Side preferred to stay in the area, and
many did indeed find housing in the public housing "projects" located at
the edge of the Lower East Side. Many others, however, could not find
housing in the area, and ended up moving far away, to other parts of the
city or even out of the city altogether.

The Movement volunteers were seeing most of the families they knew
well — people who often had participated in the Movement's programs for
years — leave the area. There were still poor people in the Lower East Side
who could take advantage of the Movement's programs, but the volunteers
also wanted to stay in touch with the families they had known for years,
and whose lives were still precarious. They needed to invent ways to do
this, and this led to the birth of the street library program.

The Street Library Program

As the poorer families left the Lower East Side, the volunteers kept in
touch with them and, whenever possible, went to visit them in their new
homes. This took the volunteers as far as Rochester, New York, and Philadelphia, Pennsylvania, as well as to all the five boroughs of New York City. The
volunteers first would go to see the family for informal, friendly visits.

For the volunteers, however, these visits were also an opportunity to
learn about other poor areas of New York City, and they would ask the family about their new neighborhood, about their neighbors, and the schools.
Often, the families encouraged the volunteers to come regularly to the
neighborhood, and even to begin programs like the ones they had done in
the Lower East Side. The volunteers were in fact eager to take the families
up on this offer, but they did not want to rush into starting programs. They
were new to these areas and wanted to take their time and get to know the
areas better, to see where they might best fit in.

The volunteers were used to working with the families' children, and
each time they would go to visit a family they brought along books for the
children to read, or activities for them to work on. The families also often
invited other children to come to the apartment to also read books with
the volunteers. From this it was a natural next step to go outside to read,
with a larger group of children. Little by little, this developed into what we
now call the street library program.

This same process took place in several areas of New York City including Coney Island and East New York in Brooklyn, and the South Bronx. The Fourth World Movement street library program in the South Bronx took place in the exact same area described so well by Jonathan Kozol in his book *Amazing Grace*.[4] In addition, the volunteers also started a street library in the Lower East Side.

The street libraries started small and simple, and grew out of the concern of Fourth World volunteers to not lose touch with very poor families who had become active members of the Fourth World network of families. The street library project was not designed in an office and later applied on the street. It grew up right on the street, and the poor families known to the volunteers were from the very beginning the architects of the project, along with the volunteers.

Today the street library program has a 15 year history in this country, and the Fourth World volunteers have developed a real expertise. Again, this expertise did not come from studying books, but rather was build up over the years, through working in close partnership with the families who participated in the street libraries. The Fourth World volunteers made great efforts to learn and draw lessons from what they were doing. For example, they all write regular journals about their activities, these journals are later reread and studied as tools for learning from action.

Street libraries take place in areas of physical devastation such as the poorest ghettoes in the city or in emergency housing areas like welfare hotels or family shelters. Life in these areas is dangerous and tense. The children of families living in these areas do not as a rule do well in school. Many are labeled as slow learners or put in special education classes — a stigma that can last for life. To the Fourth World volunteers who know them these same children are bright, curious, eager to learn. But there are obstacles in front of these children. Their life is bounded physically by their block or their immediate neighborhood; intellectually by the need to meet the constant pressures of survival; and spiritually, emotionally, and esthetically by the surrounding ugliness and violence.

The street library goes to seek out the children and their families in their own surroundings, rather than obliging the child to approach an institution that the child might see as a threat. On the street there is easy access to siblings and parents, who can come to watch the proceedings and take part in them, thus providing reinforcement to the child's interest in learning. The children feel at home in the street. It is their place, where they are free to come and go, to participate or not.

The Fourth World volunteers make sure that no one is excluded from the street library. A special effort is made to include the most resistant and those most afraid of failure. Each child, no matter how difficult it is for him or her to concentrate or to behave in a group, eventually finds a place in the street library. This insistence on including everyone is a strong message for the entire community.

Felicia, from East New York in Brooklyn, posed an especially difficult dilemma for the Fourth World volunteers, one of whom wrote the following:

> Felicia often had very old and dirty clothes, and the other children, especially the boys, constantly made fun of her. They would step away from her, saying she was dirty and smelled bad. We kept inviting and welcoming her, reading books with her and trying to ignore the comments about her. We also often had to fight so that her turn would not be taken by someone else on the computer. Our determination was a message for the other children but did not always help Felicia, because as much as we defended her, some older boys would only double their efforts to make fun of her, just to challenge us, the adults.
>
> Felicia loved to write and listen to us reading books. One year in February we had a project where the children were invited to write about famous African American men and women in a small computer database which we took around from one neighborhood to the other. Each child who wrote received a printout of his or her contribution. Felicia participated a lot and had many printouts to show. This ended up being her best defense against the other children when they wanted to exclude her. Rather than defending her, it was more efficient to praise her work in front of the other children, and to choose a project in which she could share with the others.

Stronger families in the neighborhood ask us why we continue with those who have a bad reputation. When we reply that no one should be excluded, the families usually agree and often lead us to families they know who are having an especially hard time.

Parents participate in many ways in the street libraries, but this essential partnership with the parents is not always what we expect or even hope for. We cannot necessarily expect the parents to read books and do the activities with us. This is more our job. But when parents come down to the street and sit on the stairs or a chair, their presence makes the children calmer, encourages them to participate. The presence of the parents gives us a credibility for the whole block. Parents can also monitor whether some children receive enough attention. One mother used to check our written waiting list for using the computer and remind us the following week about the children who had not gotten a chance the week before.

Reading books and storytelling is the basis of all street library activities, and books have an important place in every street library session. The following statement is from an internal document written by Bruno Tardieu.

Reading time at the street library means the children listening to stories and, for the ones who know how to read, reading on their own. I have seen children starting to read. We know the children love books. When they come first, they say they hate books. They go right away to simple drawing or building. They won't tell us for a long time that they don't know how to read. They need the other things around first. After a long time, they'll listen to a story. They think at first that, if they listen, it's a confession that they can't read. For all the children, we know the first book they enjoy because they ask for it over and over again. When they start having fun with books, that's the key. Then they learn how to read.

Books, however, are not enough; the children's imagination needs to be enlisted in a variety of ways. Music, story-telling, drawing, painting, computers, using simple tools — all further the children's participation.

Longer-term street library projects help to keep up the children's enthusiasm. One year it was the assembly of an encyclopedia containing facts the children contributed; another year it was building and decorating large flower boxes to put in front of the buildings where the children live, and yet another was the creation of a large dinosaur out of interlocking pieces of plywood. This dinosaur was displayed at several places in the community where the children live, including the local public library. Most recently, the children in New York have been working on a project about different forms of communication. They began by exploring simple tools of communication like sign language and Morse Code, listened to some other languages, visited a mail sorting facility at the local post office, and recently have begun exploring communicating with children in street libraries in other cities and other countries through the Internet.

In all these projects, books are used in conjunction with other tools — woodworking tools, art materials, computers, audio visual equipment — to permit the children to discover many aspects of the world around them. The founder of the Fourth World Movement, Father Joseph Wresinski, was a pioneer in the use of modern technology with the very poor. He wrote, "Knowledge is one of the keys to freedom, but not just any outmoded knowledge which leads nowhere. The more deprived people are, the more they need to be ahead of their time, the more they need to master the means of access to the modern world and the new culture which it is creating among people."[5]

For more than ten years, Fourth World volunteers have been using computers with children at the street libraries. This began with two old computers mounted in the back of a van. The electricity was provided by running a long extension cord from the van parked on the sidewalk through the window of one of the nearby apartments. (This is also a way that the people in the community showed their support to the street libraries, by agreeing to provide electricity for the computers.) Today the computers are still installed in the van, and they have become one of the hallmarks of the street library program.

Final Comments

The theme of street library activities can be almost anything: communication or astronomy, famous people in history or carpentry. What seems most crucial to the success of the street library is that the material be presented so that the children see that learning is fun; if the presenters are enthusiastic then the children will be as well.

Street libraries do not and should not attempt to replace essential services like public schools and public libraries. Rather, the street libraries can help to provide a spark of interest in children who otherwise would not fully take advantage of these services. The street libraries can also act as a kind of bridge between services like public libraries and certain very poor families, as the example from Coney Island demonstrated.

Finally, street libraries should not be a long-term, static project. The Fourth World Movement street libraries in New York have moved countless times over the years, following changing neighborhoods and seeking out poorer families. Ideally, once the seed of learning has been planted in a community, once key "partners" like the public libraries are free and able to reach out to the very poor, this seed should eventually be able to grow and flourish on its own, in the heart of the community.

Notes

1. American Library Association, "Library Services for the Poor." *ALA Handbook of Organization* (Chicago: American Library Association, 1996): 139–140.

2. Joseph Wresinski. *Blessed Are You the Poor* (Paris: Fourth World Publications, 1992).

3. Robert Kraus. *Leo the Late Bloomer* (New York: Schuster for Young Readers, 1987).

4. Jonathan Kozol. *Amazing Grace: The Lives of Children and the Conscience of a Nation* (New York: Crown, 1995).

5. Vincent Fanelli. *The Human Face of Poverty* (New York: Bootstrap Press, 1990).

For Further Reading

French Economic and Social Council. *Chronic Poverty and Lack of Basic Security. Reporter Joseph Wresinski.* Landover, Md.: Fourth World Publications, 1994. (Translation from the French, "Grande Pauvreté et Précarité Économique et Sociale," originally published by the Official Journal of the Republic of France, February, 1987.)

International Movement ATD Fourth World. *The Family Album.* Paris: Editions Quart Monde, 1994.

de Vos van Steenwijk, Alwine. *Father Joseph Wresinski: Voice of the Poorest.* Santa Barbara, Calif.: Queenship Press, 1996.

Hosmer Branch Library

BY WIZARD MARKS

Never doubt that a small group of thoughtful, committed citizens can change the world; indeed, it's the only thing that ever has.
— Margaret Mead

In October, 1997 the newly enlarged, refurbished and remodeled-to-historic-standard Hosmer Branch of the Minneapolis Public Library reopened. It had been one long, lonely year without it. At the same time, it represents a considerable victory for the cluster of eight neighborhoods who use Hosmer. What follows is a story of one economically disadvantaged neighborhood's struggle to keep their local library.

In the spring of 1992, then Mayor Donald Fraser and Eighth Ward City Councilwoman (now Mayor) Sharon Sayles Belton held three meetings in an attempt to sell the notion of closing down both Hosmer and Roosevelt branch libraries and building a regional library in their place.

Each of the three meetings was packed with neighborhood people; particularly community elders who made a point of turning out in great numbers. Councilwoman Sayles Belton, who conducted the meetings, heard, in sometimes angry, sometimes mystified, sometimes disappointed voices that the residents were solidly against the idea. The proposed regional library, even though the councilwoman hinted it would be as close as two blocks from Hosmer's address at 36th Street and Fourth Avenue was a resounding "no sale."

The elders, all of whom address the councilwoman as Sharon, were particularly vocal about their objections. They expressed three points of objection. First and foremost, the Hosmer library building represented the only remaining public building in the Central neighborhood which was still a community gathering place operated for its intended use. The junior high school had been abandoned by the school board and rescued by those same seniors, led by Clarissa Walker, to become Sabathani Community Center. Central High School had been abandoned, then left unattended so that its pipes burst in the annual sub-zero winter and, finally, had to be torn down, an outcome which still rankles many residents.

Second, Hosmer is a Carnegie library built in 1911, a little architectural gem with crenelated watchtowers on two corners. Hosmer's appearance alone makes it the focus of a lot of imaginative play among neighborhood children. Hosmer has three fireplaces, a skylight, and, though closed off, a balcony up a tiny, winding staircase which once served as the librarian's office. The windows cover the outer walls and are set about six feet off the floor, the first six feet being covered with built-in oak book shelves.

Third, having seen North Regional Library, the existing regional library, many residents were not at all enchanted with its streamlined, modern architecture and its feeling of being very businesslike, rather than intimate. Roosevelt Branch's users would insist that a new library be closer to them. This would be a hardship on the elders, many of whom consider Hosmer Library as their recreation since they don't have the money to take taxis or the energy to do a two or three bus transfer to get to the library. Even in deep winter, when the weather is thoroughly nasty, they can walk a block or two to Hosmer to interact with other humans in person in an atmosphere they enjoy, which costs nothing, and which is safe, comfortable, and interesting.

The alternative "suggestion" put forward by neighborhood people was to use city money instead to refurbish Hosmer library, keeping its character intact, but enlarging it as well. Maintaining the character of the neighborhood has been a fifteen year and continuing struggle for Central neighborhood which is home to Hosmer. The city has, in a variety of its functions, behaved in such a way as to disinvest in this inner city neighborhood. For many years, it allowed pornography stores to dominate commercial nodes, had torn down houses willy-nilly, had crisscrossed the center of the neighborhood with one-way streets to accommodate people working downtown and living south of the area or wanting to jump on the freeway from neighborhoods east of Central, the freeway being Central's western border.

Banks had red-lined the area and, to too large an extent, still do. Insurance companies well as practiced red-lining. The city itself through its development agency and its public housing authority have practiced redlining by buying up homes cheaply, and either turning them into scattered site housing for the poor or boarding them for demolition and letting them sit for years. Boarded homes are preyed on by thieves who steal copper pipe, windows, woodwork, fixtures, built-ins, fireplace surrounds, and bric-a-brac.

The neighborhoods are slowly forcing changes, but bad habits and poor practices are very difficult to change, particularly after the name "ghetto" becomes attached to an area. (Police officers, some of the most egregious offenders, regularly call Central the ghetto.)

It is true that "ghetto" when applied to deteriorating neighborhoods in Minneapolis does not resonate as it does when applied to New York, Chicago, Miami or Los Angeles. There are only four million people in the state and only half of them live in the Twin Cities metropolitan area (defined as seven counties); Minneapolis has roughly 360,000.

However, two prostitution saunas have been allowed to continue operating, one for 25 years, and street prostitutes work the corners on the north side of the neighborhood. The onset of crack had created an intolerable situation with killings, huge numbers of street prostitutes, drug houses and open market drug dealing, and children neglected if not actively abused by crack using or multi-addicted parents. While that situation is changing ever so slowly, one can easily see how residents would be willing to pull out the stops to save Hosmer library as it represents an "easier" time.

The Central neighborhood experienced not only white flight, but middle class flight. When homeowners could no longer get a fair price to sell, they began renting out their beautiful old homes. Soon the neighborhood was no longer dominated by homeowners but by renters. The stability and cohesion of the neighborhood was severely compromised. When tax changes in the 1980s made rental property less lucrative, speculators moved in, buying out ex-residents' rental homes. Money was not focused on maintaining those homes any longer, but on breaking them up into apartments and "rooming houses," many of the latter used as sites for prostitution. Then crack hit in 1988.

Hosmer itself had been badly used by the Minneapolis Public Library system. Hosmer is but one of probably scores, if not hundreds of examples nationwide of the consequences of disinvestment in inner city neighborhoods. This is not to say that the public library system intentionally set out to disinvest in Hosmer and five other inner city branches. But it does say that members of the library board did not see any red flags when presented with a plan which would hugely disadvantage an inner city neighborhood.

The library chose to apply the information they got on usage statistics during the years of disinvestment in a negative fashion. Instead of saying, for example, "Good lord, our statistics are dropping, can we reverse this decline?" the library and administration decided to shift from a community library to a "browsing library" some fifteen years ago. They apparently reasoned that since usage was down and patrons were asking for recent novels, they would concentrate on that. Resources shifted from the usual materials which keep a library strong to paperback novels. The reasoning at the time was that Hosmer's statistics did not show enough usage to merit a full-service library. This reasoning became a self-fulfilling prophecy.

Using statistics to justify withdrawal of resources is disastrous in poorer neighborhoods because it creates a downward spiral of expectations on the parts of both the library and its users. Fewer people use a library which does not have resources to satisfy customer need. Those symbiotic bad decisions, to invest in paperback novels and base budget resources on the percentage of users is particularly galling in light of the fact that the mission of the Carnegie public libraries was and still is to level the playing field between the poor and the middle classes by providing resources poor families could not afford but which could improve their lives. Libraries in poorer neighborhoods should have as many resources as the residents need and the building will hold because children must learn to dream their way out of poverty in order to get out of poverty, and their parents must do likewise. Libraries have resources to help people consider the possibilities of the world outside their narrow sphere.

As Hosmer's statistics fell further and further, books walked away in greater numbers without being checked out or through not being returned — 25 percent in 1995. Families with few resources and somewhat transient lives due to lack of money keep books out beyond their due dates and then could not afford to return them and pay the fines. Hosmer's theft/loss statistics climbed as people were too proud to ask for fine waivers.

The library became an unwitting instrument of class warfare. Once the library colludes in the process of ghettoizing an inner city neighborhood it becomes an instrument of the middle class to hoard resources for branches in more middle class areas and further entrench hard core poverty. Poverty is more than a lack of money, it is a lack of all kinds of resources, access to resources, and entry to decision making. Finally, in a neighborhood where features of the landscape, both interior and exterior, are literally stolen off the buildings, buildings are ripped out of the landscape. Houses are boarded. Trash fills the gutters and blows around the yards. Poverty becomes a crushing sensory deprivation which hampers the mind from imagining a different place, a different life, or even a different breakfast.

In any event, the library recognized its mistake and began the work of changing that policy and reversing the results of the policy with the advent of Roy Woodstrom as librarian in 1994. Roy, knowing that remodeling was imminent, argued to Ann Christensen, district librarian and supervisor of several libraries, that it would help to budget more resources to Hosmer because the branch would have to have a larger number of volumes and all other library resources to sustain the larger space.

In 1993, Sharon Sayles Belton took office not only as the first woman mayor of Minneapolis, but the first African American woman mayor of any city in the country. She carried the ball to focus the Capital Long Range Improvement Committee (CLIC) of the city on finding the over $2 million it would take to enlarge and refurbish Hosmer Library. The two million plus in CLIC money was earmarked to be devoted entirely to physical improvements of Hosmer, to guard its historical visage, be larger, and be more convenient for both staff and users.

Concurrently, the city's Neighborhood Revitalization Program (NRP) was directing tax increment money into neighborhood coffers. City agencies, including the library, were directed in the language of the NRP's founding document (originally called the "Twenty Year Plan") to start from the proposition that neighborhoods would "direct the services of city agencies." Central neighborhood received almost $6 million in seed money, with instructions to collaborate and leverage the seed money. Surrounding neighborhoods, some with far lower allocations of funds, were also going through the planning process of the NRP. Central devoted approximately $140,000 and other neighborhoods devoted differing amounts until we achieved over $200,000.

The architectural firm of Meyer, Sherer, & Rockcastle, Ltd., was hired. They have done historic preservation work, particularly of libraries, and they were willing to work with a member of the Historic Preservation Commission to check their designs against the historic standard.

When Hosmer opened in the fall of 1997, her three fireplaces had been converted to gas fires (fire laws have changed) but they retained their beautiful surrounds. The Arts and Crafts era library tables, plain oak, straight-legged tables with brass "socks," had been stripped and refinished. The grand stairway had been returned to the center of the entry and the required elevator moved to the side. The skylight above the entry was uncovered from its coats of paint. Two stained glass windows had been installed, one in the transom over the front door and one on the new south wall along the same axis. Comfortable chairs more representative of the era (1911) in which Hosmer was built sit around the fireplaces. The librarian has an office to call his own. There is a room for library staff to repair books. There are bathrooms on the main floor, two small study carrels and a small conference room. A new children's room has a glass wall to contain the greater noise and give small children more room. Youth and young adults have an entire "room" to themselves. There is a reference desk! A new phone and computer system and enough terminals accompany the change, as well as Internet access.

Central and Bryant neighborhoods (Bryant's borders begin two blocks south of Hosmer) decided to devote some $143,000 in NRP money to create a computer training program in Hosmer Library's old community room. The funding budgeted for a three year, full-time equivalent position for a teacher to train neighborhood people on the use of the equipment and software. Some software is to be devoted to access the State Employment Office's job listings, help people create resumes, and create a kid's employment webpage.

Since that decision was made in the latter half of 1995, Roy Woodstrom and Ann Christensen have gone to the people of other neighborhoods who use Hosmer and asked them to devote some of their NRP resources to Hosmer. At this point about another $58,000 in resources have come to Hosmer to support library initiatives, particularly for children, youth, and young adults.

Because Central residents have nine different languages and two to three times that many dialects among those languages, residents have created, with a small endowment, the Lorraine O. Berman fund for multicultural materials for children and youth.

Having solidified building, library resources, computers and trainer, the struggle was not quite finished. For many years, Hosmer has been open only five days per week (closed Fridays and Sundays). This too is a way to insure that usage drops off and stays low. When encountered at other libraries, neighborhood people have said they want to use a library which is open six days a week and which has better resources than Hosmer has had.

The neighborhoods clearly stated that they would put the additional NPR money into Hosmer if it would stay open six days a week. At this point, with opening day less than a month away, the library will be open six days a week, though Saturday hours are still attenuated. The neighborhood will have to carry the onus of making sure that library usage goes up a good deal in order to demand longer hours. Other branches have as much as another 20 hours per week. There is confidence among residents that Hosmer will have the usage to justify increased hours at the end of a year's experience in the newly refurbished building.

The staff of Minneapolis Public Library has realized that the larger library will also require a larger staff and has agreed to an increase. Because of the diversity of residents and the under-representation by people of color among library aides and librarians, Central residents believe it would be very helpful to have at least one person of color on staff. To insure that no backsliding happens, the area representative to the library board has been asked to give some assurances and to keep a keen eye on board resolutions to make sure that Hosmer's requirements are met.

Throughout this process, neighborhood residents have had much more contact with the library board than previously. It has been an eye-opening and disappointing series of discoveries. The one person of color on the board was treated disrespectfully by her colleagues. That member is the representative from the Hosmer neighborhoods.

An eye-opening event was the board's response to the neighborhood's request that Hosmer be designated as a historical preservation. In 1992, when the notion of creating a regional library was first suggested, the neighborhood began researching and found that historical designation had not been granted in 1980 when first requested by the Central neighborhood. The Historical Preservation Commission recommended preservation status to the City Council in 1996. At the hearing in 1997, the library board, unwarrantedly concerned about the possible cost and ignoring the vocalized concerns of the neighborhood, did not request preservation status for Hosmer. They justified this request by stating that their constituents wanted them to make the best use of library funds and that historic preservation would be expensive.

The library board was resistant throughout the process to hearing neighborhood concerns. It was also unwilling to hear that its information was not accurate, nor was it willing to change when it was presented with correct information. The spirit of neighborhood revitalization was not one with which they were prepared to grapple. The notion that "neighborhoods would direct the services of the city and its agencies" was difficult to accept.

Guiding the public library requires elasticity; what is needed is a sense of inclusiveness and welcoming to the wide variety of people who libraries serve. For any board to act rigidly is a disservice to the city's library system and, consequently, to the city's residents. It is yet a reminder that even though people suffer from systemic class and race bias, those biases are exercised by individuals. It means that individuals have to change or be voted out of office. Voters have to examine candidates for office on their ability to be responsive to the needs of the community and their ability to debate the issues in an open forum and make changes in the practices of the institution in response to community concerns.

After lots of hard work and effort on the part of many individuals, the victory that is Hosmer Library opened on October 4, 1997, with the subdued fanfare typical of libraries. It is beautiful and it has almost twice the floor space and books and materials.

The neighborhood has been planning to ask for even more materials, but is not asking the library to provide them. Also, the neighborhood would like to install two pianos of the type which can only be heard through headphones so that a music teacher can give lessons there for people in the neighborhoods. Two residents have donated works of art to Hosmer. Through the neighborhood's "Intergenerational Dialog" group, they hope to encourage older adults and youth to read to younger children on a regular basis at the library. Above all, the neighborhood wants to encourage learning among its children so that they can create fulfilling lives for themselves and their families.

SUGGESTIONS
FOR ACTION

Ways to Make a Difference

BY SHERRY LAMPMAN

Changes in our country's government programs that provide assistance to poor people are giving states authority to reconfigure their own safety net provisions. Discussions about public assistance programs will be more frequent at the local level, and it is essential that members of the public have good information on hand to make informed judgments about the redesign of our social welfare programs. Librarians and library staff are at the front lines of the information flow, and as stewards of information, it behooves them to be sure the public has ready access to the facts, opinions, strategy discussions, theories, and proposals that are the heart of public policy development. Librarians and library staff also have information available that could ease the transition of people who are receiving some forms of public assistance into situations where they will need to be self-sufficient.

These are just a few simple steps librarians and library staff can take to enrich the public discussion and make a contribution to their communities. These ideas were offered as part of a program at the October, 1996, Minnesota Library Association's Annual Conference entitled "Women, Children, and Poverty: What's the Connection and What Does It Mean to Libraries?"

Keep a few facts handy. When the discussion comes round to poverty, be sure people know what the federal poverty guidelines are.

1996 Federal Poverty Guidelines
(For people living in the 48 contiguous states and D.C.)

Number in Family	Poverty level
1	$ 7,740
2	10,360
3	12,980
4	15,600
5	18,220
6	20,840
7	23,460
8	26,080

(Source: *Federal Register*, vol. 61, no. 43, March 4, 1996)

Help people learn about the resources that are there for them...

For most poor families, the primary need is money. Many times, it's not education about family finances or family budgeting that's necessary, because there's not enough money to make a budget. It's getting money into families' hands that's important, whether in the form of wages, tax refunds, child care subsidies, or benefit programs.

For example, provide and display information on federal and state tax credits. Just a few years ago, it was estimated that 20,000 Minnesota working families were missing out on $17 to $18 million because they weren't filing for the Earned Income Tax Credit, most likely because they didn't know about it. In some cases, this meant thousands of dollars sitting in Washington not going to families it was meant for. We heard stories of people saving their homes from mortgage foreclosure because of the money they received back from tax refunds; one family bought their first used car; another paid medical bills. For the 1995 tax year, over 212,000 Minnesotans filed for the federal Earned Income Credit and state Working Family Credit to the tune of nearly $290 million!

Actively seek job applicants from organizational partners that serve poor people. For example, the St. Paul Public Library's compact with Head Start provides that they share job notices. Post job notices from community partners. Have a job notice area in a prominent place in the library. Have job counselors come in for public sessions once or twice a week. Publicize availability of the library's job counseling sessions in places where people go— community centers, shelters, social service agencies, churches, grocery stores, laundromats, literacy programs, child care centers.

Help people save money....

For example, people who are eligible for the Earned Income Tax Credit (those working families with incomes up to the mid–$20,000s) can get free tax assistance at hundreds of VITA (Volunteer Income Tax Assistance) sites across the state.

Advocate for the elimination or reduction of library fines.

Library staff can also help activist groups and organizations and their clients get out their messages. Many low-budget groups have no money for marketing; they have to be creative — why not lend a hand by offering to host an event, displaying posters, distributing flyers.

Help families become self-sufficient...

Provide and promote availability of resources — educational, work-related, job-seeking, family economics — to families and organizations serving poor people.

Provide information on women's and family health issues in basic, easy to read, easily accessible formats.

Provide teen services — films, social groups, homework help, tutoring.

Sponsor a free tax help program at your library. Recruit volunteers from your staff to become trained VITA tax preparers. Help tax filers find ways to save money, show them how to keep records to support their deductions and credits.

Help the organizations working with low-income families...

Build partnerships with organizations in your community that serve low-income families; tell those organizations what you have, how the library works, update them on new materials and services.

Ask those organizations what issues they're working on. What are their greatest challenges? How can the library make a contribution to their work? Libraries have the information — demographics, announcements of special events, notice of new businesses moving into the area, public meeting schedules, new materials pertinent to a hot issue – that could make a big difference to small community organizations. What role could the library play in just providing information on fundraising, on what foundations are doing, on what corporations are focusing on? The librarian could be the scanner and information "mentor" for an organization and thereby indirectly contribute to the improvement of the lives of the people being served by the organization.

Help eliminate poverty...

As individual citizens, challenge public policy, and as librarians, provide ready access to information and opinions on public policy that is being publicly debated — especially policies that affect low-income people such as welfare reform, cutting tax credits, reducing food stamps, eliminating benefits to immigrants, health benefits, and so on. From "The Environmentalist's Guide to the Public Library" by Andrew Koebrick and commissioned by Libraries for the Future:

> A broad public understanding of the important issues of the day allows citizens to elect representatives who best serve their interests, and when coupled with a popular willingness to protest, an educated public can confront and change social and political problems.

Collect, display, and make readily accessible current and up-to-date information on issues that are being debated such as the wage gap, lack of jobs, lack of child care, and welfare reform. People need to make informed judgments — whether at the voting place, or in the process of influencing public policy or communicating with legislators.

Invite local organizations working on specific issues to develop fact sheets that can be kept in special files — the library does not have to endorse the ideas, but at least people will have access to a variety of viewpoints.

Sponsor public events (such as forums, speakers, community discussions, presentations by local organizations) so people can understand issues affecting them — taxes, child care options, job gap, corporate welfare, crime, school services, and others.

For example, after you get the annual updated Kids Count Data Book, invite a representative from the Children's Defense Fund of Minnesota or a child advocate from Congregations Concerned for Children to lead a discussion based on data for your county. Talk about things the average person can do to make a difference.

Endorse public events — such as the Minnesota Library Association did for Minnesota's Stand for Children event on June 1, 1996.

Develop displays that highlight the most pertinent materials on welfare

reform: magazine articles, upcoming speakers, radio and television programs, conferences, workshops, community gatherings, news exposés,
special studies. Help people get the information they need to become part
of the discussion; help people get the information they need to help shape
the public policy before it becomes law.

Examine in advance and have available for public perusal any documents developed by local groups proposing policies related to welfare
reform. For example, Minnesota's "Affirmative Options for Welfare Reform
Group," representing a wide range of organizations concerned for the well-
being of poor people, developed a set of "Minnesota Principles for Responsible Economic and Community Support Strategies" that was presented
and endorsed by the Minnesota Library Association at its annual business
meeting. The Association agreed to let all its membership know about the
principles by printing them in its member newsletter. This is just one way
of expanding the number of people discussing the ideas behind welfare
reform strategies.

Have a special area for reports, brochures, and newsletters of local
organizations; have files on local organizations, addresses, contact names,
and purpose of groups so that interested people can get involved.

Provide easy to understand guides (written at a basic level) on how to
influence public policy, on how to work with legislators, on what organizations are doing what.

Examine your own library's mission statement — who is supposed to
be served? Are all people welcome? Are all people being served? What are
the barriers to people using the library? What steps could be taken to eliminate those barriers?

Think systems — who's determining your library's policies? Work, as
a citizen, to assure people know how library policies are determined, how
people are elected or appointed to library boards, what channels people
need to use in order to affect policies. What are library policies for working *with* the community? How can they be adapted, changed so they provide for working *with* the community, not just *for* or *on behalf* of the community?

Contribute to efforts to assure that children know how to read and
are encouraged to read. Emphasize that reading is essential to future success; do whatever you can to be sure children are given the assistance they
need to develop their potentials.

Work with local literacy providers to publicize availability of Adult
Basic Education classes, GED, ESL, and the like, to help adults improve their
literacy skills.

10 Reasons Why ...

BY JOSHUA COHEN

... A Person Who Works with People Who Are Homeless Would Use a Library

1. Government reports
2. Legislation, rights, laws
3. Funding sources and information
4. Demographic information
5. Instructional materials
6. Current events in the field
7. Latest research in the field
8. Maps, phone books, directories
9. Subject searches and reference questions
10. Special programs

... A Person Who Is Homeless Would Use a Library

1. Community information and referral services
2. Regional guides and newspapers
3. Job search/career guidance
4. Quiet study environment
5. Educational/vocational courses information

6. Programs for children
7. Literacy/ESL tutoring
8. New reader/foreign language materials
9. Adult programs
10. Audiovisual materials

PROGRAMS IN SHELTERS AND PUBLIC HOUSING

Libraries and the Poor: What's the Connection?

BY MILDRED DOTSON AND YOLANDA BONITCH

The library is the university of the poor. It is the intellectual lifeline of the poor. The New York Public Library is an organization which, by its history and nature, serves to overcome socioeconomic and racial biases. This is particularly important in New York City, where so many residents face multiple barriers that impede their full participation in economic and social life, including low educational levels, and limited literacy skills. The NYPL is especially committed to serving the disadvantaged user who lacks the resources to access information elsewhere. The Office of Special Services of the Library is committed to developing library outreach programs for nonusers, the underserved, and people with special needs. Yes, there is a connection. There are many connections. The real question is, How do we make the connections work?

The faces of the poor are many and they are not always easy to identify. Some of the poor are nearly invisible while others are obvious and their needs are numerous. The most visible are people on public assistance and people without homes. These groups, however, include individuals who are not easily recognizable as "the poor"—these include adult non-readers, immigrants (especially the non–English-speaking), older adults, and inmates in correctional facilities.

New York City is a city of approximately 7.3 million people, 28 percent of whom were born in other countries. Poverty in the city in 1995 increased by 37 percent since 1989. Some of the poor live in substandard housing; some share living space with friends or relatives. Still others have suitable living quarters but because the rent is so high, they live at a survival level. Since 1989 the number of family members without homes, living in temporary housing facilities, grew to over 17,000 from almost 13,000. The number of adults dropped to 6,000 from over 9,000. This number does not include the people living on the streets who do not receive services from shelters. In 1996 the number of homeless families in temporary housing increased over the previous year. Emergency housing for single adults also saw an increase over the number for 1995.[1]

In New York City since 1989, there has been a slight increase in the number of people on public assistance; over half a million adults and over half a million children concentrated mostly in northern Manhattan, Harlem, the South Bronx and eastern Brooklyn. There are poor in many other parts of the city but the majority reside in these areas. Based on 1990 Census data and 1993 income support data, problems in these areas are "rooted in economic distress," with as high as 42 percent of all residents living below the federally-defined poverty level and receiving some income support. The New York City poverty rate for children increased from 31.8 percent to 38.5 percent from 1979 to 1992. The number of poor children in the city grew from 551,533 to 661,700, an increase of more than 110,000 children. The elderly poverty rate in the city increased from 14.4 percent to 19.8 percent . Each year the total elderly population includes more minority elderly who are at a greater risk of poverty than the white elderly. Furthermore, an increasing number of the elderly are beyond age 85, when they are at greater risk of poverty.[2]

The needs of all of these persons are as individual as our own. How libraries respond to these needs depends on many elements — institutional commitment, staff training and sensitivity, and resources. The New York Public Library has a longstanding commitment to developing services for all New Yorkers. Successful collaboration and networks with community agencies, intensive staff training and the commitment of on-going funding have enabled the library to provide innovative programs for the poor.

The summer of 1986 saw the New York Public Library initiate a service to shelters for people without homes, a service which has continued to grow. Throughout the 1980s, the height of the homeless problem in New York City, the library provided programs and services for 25 shelters. Although NYPL's involvement in providing services to people living in transitional housing includes people of all ages, the library's organized outreach to people living in shelters began with children. Other agencies were already working with the adults in the shelter, but the needs of the children were not being met. In 1986 local Community Planning Board 5, which covers the West Side of central Manhattan, requested that New York Public Library offer library service for the children at the Martinique Hotel. Housing families in the Martinique was part of a major effort of the city to find temporary housing for the growing numbers of families living on the street. The hotel, a large shelter in Midtown Manhattan, was not close to any neighborhood branch libraries.

Through collaboration with the Single Parents Resource Center, the Children's Aid Society, and the Hudson Guild, NYPL's Office of Special Services responded by setting up a series of weekly storytime sessions during that summer. At 9:30 a.m. every day of the program, the outreach librarian knocked on doors to remind parents about the 10:30 a.m. storytime. Sleepy parents would open the door and when they heard the message, they would give a positive and grateful response, and promise to send the children down as soon as they were dressed. Some of the children arrived in their best clothes. The storytime sessions were conducted by children's librarians who read stories, sang songs, taught origami, and used their creativity and love of books to introduce children to the wonderful world of books. Deposit collections of books for children, teenagers and adults were provided at the shelter on permanent loan so that all could borrow them and enjoy them in their rooms. Parents were invited to accompany the children to the recreation area for the weekly program. A special event was planned for the last session: a puppet show, or magic show or ventriloquism, in addition to fun prizes which were given to all who attended. The entire summer program proved to be a successful way to reach the parents.

In December 1986 the New York Public Library received the Eleanor Roosevelt Community Service Award for its services at the hotel. The program continued until the hotel closed three years later. It was later expanded to other shelters in the Bronx, Manhattan and Staten Island.

Outreach to men's and women's shelters followed a different path depending on the requests of the shelter activities' directors. Discarded books in good condition are much appreciated by the shelter residents and this service is usually accompanied by some type of library orientation, including a description of resources found at local and specialized libraries: special collections, job information sources, English classes for speakers of other languages and basic literacy instruction. Tours to local libraries are arranged whenever the support of shelter staff is available.

A very different type of library program, "Read-to-Me," is an example of networking among four agencies: the city, the library, New York Cares (a volunteer organization) and family shelters. In 1989 the New York City's Human Resources Administration asked New York Public Library to participate in a program already in existence at one branch of the Queens

Borough Public Library. Once a month on Saturdays a group of volunteers from New York Cares, a well-known and well-administrated volunteer organization, brought children from a family shelter to the local branch library. If the library was not within walking distance, the city provided bus transportation. At the library, the children's librarian read several stories to the group and the rest of the morning was spent by the children and volunteers enjoying books together. The time given to sharing books was to be the heart of the program. For some children this would be the only time that an adult would share stories and books with them. The volunteers often introduced the children to the books which had been their favorites when they were young. The enjoyment on both sides was always evident — nostalgia on one side and discovery on the other.

The original "Read-to-Me" program was located at the George Bruce Branch Library with children from the Convent Avenue Family Center in Harlem . The children arrived at 10 a.m. and stayed at the library until 3:30 p.m. After the morning storytime and book sharing activities, the children and volunteers went to the auditorium and enjoyed bag lunches provided by the volunteers. The rest of the afternoon was engaged in a special event or performance arranged by the Human Resources Administration.

The program proved to be very successful. The children looked forward to the monthly Saturday session with the volunteers, and the volunteers, in turn, were very enthusiastic at being able to become "buddies" to the children. Some teenagers from the shelter at times attended the "Read-to-Me" and they were given the choice of either listening to the children's stories or going directly to the Young Adult area in the library to find books of their liking. Inevitably the teens chose to listen to the stories first and then go to the Young Adult area with their New York Cares buddy.

The success of the first year of the "Read-to-Me" program spurred the city to expand the program to other libraries and shelters. This required an adjustment in the program schedule. Most branch libraries could not accommodate an all-day program, and so it was agreed to concentrate on the morning session, from 10 to noon. The volunteers still bring bag lunches for the children, but the food is eaten elsewhere. The city and the New York Cares volunteers are responsible for the afternoon activities either at the shelter or at another location. At present there are three branch libraries in Manhattan and one in the Bronx that are sites for the program. Periodically the agencies involved evaluate the program in order to improve it and to expand it further. At one point a shelter had to be excluded due to lack of cooperation on the part of the shelter staff. This proves the importance of the human element, staff dedication and input in networking. Unless the staff of each agency supports and encourages the program, it cannot work.

These programs were supported by funds from the federal Library Services and Construction Act Title I grants and continues to be supported by the New York State Coordinated Outreach Services grant. The New York Public Library has made a difference in the lives of some people without homes. As a single agency working alone, it would have been difficult to achieve success, but working in conjunction with other agencies has assured follow-through, on-going creativity and continuity.

The New York Public Library's literacy program, Centers for Reading and Writing, supports the educational goals of adult nonreaders who are primarily poor. The library began offering free adult literacy tutoring in collaboration with Literacy Volunteers of New York in 1977 at four branch libraries as part of an LSCA initiative. In 1984, the New York City Adult Literacy Initiative was created to expand and improve upon education services available to adults with limited reading, writing, math and English-language proficiency. The New York Public Library established eight Centers for Reading and Writing in eight branches. The eight Centers were renovated to provide comfortable and supportive environments for adults returning to school. Collections of print and nonprint materials appropriate for adult beginning readers were developed and made available to students in the program.

The Centers serve adults living in communities where the poverty rate is as high as 51.5 percent and more than half of the residents are unemployed or underemployed. According to the *Statement of Needs* for Community District 4 in the Bronx, "Our library branches provide a strong secondary support for the educational needs of the people of our district as well as adding to their limited recreational activities."

The Centers for Reading and Writing offer adult students access to free comprehensive educational options and resources that include small group instruction in reading and writing provided by volunteer tutors, Adult Basic Education classes, computer-assisted instruction, collections of print materials for adult new readers, collections of software and video materials, class visits, and enrichment activities and outings. The Centers emphasize a holistic, learner-centered approach to reading and writing instruction using a curriculum designed to reflect the needs and interest of adults and the learning differences of a diverse ethnic student population. The adult students are provided with many opportunities to participate in program planning and development. Students have the opportunity to act as advocates for the program by addressing the City Council and attending Community Board meetings. Journals of student writings reveal the impact that the literacy program has made on this lives. One student says,

One of my greatest experiences in life is to be back in school. I have so many regrets in my education. Most of all, what bothers me is when my children have their homework and I cannot help them. We learn from other people. When I miss class it worries me, but as a single parent I have to work.... At times I do not have a token.

New York City is increasingly a city of immigrants, many of whom need basic literacy training, English language skills, and workforce preparedness. *The Newest New Yorkers*,[3] a 1996 report released recently by the New York City Department of City Planning, found that immigration was 32 percent higher in the 1990s than in the 1980s particularly from the Hispanic Caribbean, the former Soviet Union, Mexico, Africa and South America. The Washington Heights neighborhood, in particular, was one of three neighborhoods in the city to attract the most immigrants between the years 1990 and 1994: 28,000 — 82 percent of whom were from the Dominican Republic. These statistics are particularly important in light of the recent study by the Census Bureau that shows that the median household income rose for every American ethnic and racial group except for the country's 27 million Hispanic residents, for whom the figure fell 5.1 percent. Researchers point to a number of factors to explain this decline, including fewer well-paying blue-collar jobs and a widening gap between Hispanic students and others in high school and college graduation rates (Hispanics have the highest dropout rate of any group in the country). Researchers also point to language skills as the most critical barrier to success. A significant proportion of the population is semiliterate or illiterate, with English being a second language for much of the adult population. Working age residents are poor and dislocated, and many are unskilled and unemployed.

Adult education and access to English as a Second Language classes is increasingly important as a result of the recent changes in federal welfare laws requiring recipients to move into employment within two years and new immigration regulations. English classes for immigrants have been available in the Library since 1914, when classes were offered in association with the Young Men's and Young Women's Christian Association at 16 branch libraries for adults speaking Italian, Russian, Hungarian, Yiddish, Bohemian, Polish and Lettish. Since 1983, the Library, in collaboration with the Riverside Language Program, has offered ESL classes geared to non–English-speaking adults who need to develop basic conversational skills. The program targets immigrants living in the poorest communities of the city and whose English language proficiency is at the lowest level. Although the majority of the ESL students work, they can be classified as the working poor because they work in jobs that pay below the minimum wage.

Thirty-three classes at 13 branch libraries are offered in the day, evening and on Saturday to adults age 16 or older. The two largest immigrant groups served by the Library's ESL program are Spanish-speaking students (63 percent) and Russian-speaking students (11 percent). In addition, the library has a multimedia language learning center at the Aguilar Branch where students receive individualized or small group instruction in English by using multimedia personal computers, video and audio tapes. In addition, the Junior Lions, a library volunteer organization, provides English instruction for immigrants at the advanced to intermediate levels of English language proficiency.

Anecdotes from the ESL teachers tell the story of the impact of the program on the lives of the adults that participate in the classes:

> Paul from Peru has two jobs as a stock person. He works seven days a week and studies English at home for two hours every day. His English has improved noticeably every class. On the last day of class, he presented me with four perfectly filled out job applications. He is planning to bus tables at a large hotel restaurant in Manhattan. After that, he plans to become a waiter and make big tips. He will!

From a student:

> I came from China, and I have been here for a year. This English program is very important for me. I really appreciate it. When I came here, I didn't know how to speak English. I went to the library in the first level class, then the second and then the fourth. After I almost finished this class I knew my English had improved because I took the TOEFL [Test of English as a Foreign Language]. I thank you for these classes. Thanks to every teacher who has ever taught me.

The funding for these programs come from a variety of sources. Primary funding for the literacy program, the Centers for Reading and Writing, and the ESL program comes from New York City Adult Literacy Initiative. The Initiative funds are allocated by the Mayor's Office of Adult Literacy to the three library systems in the city, the City University of New York, the Board of Education and community-based organizations to provide educational opportunities for adults returning to school. In addition, the library uses the New York State Coordinated Outreach Services grant, New York State Adult Literacy Funds, and until recently federal Library Services and Construction Act Title I and Title VI grants. Private funders have also provided generous support for these programs. They include the Robert Wood Johnson, Jr., Charitable Trust, the Lila Wallace–Reader's Digest Fund, the Mellon Family Foundation, Banco Santander, the Uris Brothers Fund, and the St. James Episcopal Church Fund.

The library also provides services to prison detainees, inmates and ex-offenders in 21 city jails and six state pre-release centers. Research has shown that the majority of inmates are African Americans and Hispanics who have low literacy skills, do not have a high school diploma, are unskilled and live in poverty. Library services provide inmates with resources for self-study as well as recreational outlets. Library services include deposits of book collections for general libraries, cultural programs, career and education workshops. The library publishes the pamphlet *Connections VI: A Guide for Ex-Inmates and the Job Search Guide*.[4] This pamphlet is distributed free of charge to ex-inmates, probation and parole officers and other libraries in New York State. *Connections* is written and edited by the Institutional Librarian and provides inmates with information on resources in housing, education, health, family services, financial and legal assistance and social and cultural resources. *The Job Search Guide* is a guide for ex-inmates to the step involved in finding employment. *The Guide* covers interviewing, resume writing, provides advise on job discrimination and practice job applications. These services are made available through state funding.

The three components necessary for successful innovative programs that have a positive impact on the city's poorest residents require a commitment by the library to train its staff to deliver these services. The Office of Special Services, responsible for developing outreach services for the 84 branches of the New York Public Library, has a staff training program that (1) documents for the staff the demographics of the population, (2) sensitizes the staff to the different needs of the various groups, (3) engages the staff in learning to develop, implement, promote and evaluate programs, (4) assists the staff in outreach efforts and (5) provides a framework for networking and collaborating with government agencies, community organizations and advocacy groups. The training includes:

The Outreach Specialty Seminar: Four sessions which examine the history of outreach, the library's mission to serve the disadvantaged, current programs, services and collection development that specifically address the information and reading needs of the targeted populations, and methods of developing networks and collaborations. This seminar, offered yearly for 20 librarians, heightens participants' awareness of and sensitivity to the needs of the target populations and provides guidelines for developing and evaluating programs and collections.

Outreach Specialty Meetings: Held twice a year for 70 librarians, these meetings provide branch staff with a forum to review, discuss and focus on an outreach topic. Past meetings have focused on:

- Selecting and Purchasing Foreign Language Materials
- Changing Ideas–New Frontiers: Serving People with Disabilities
- Learning, Thinking, Helping: The "Keys" to Healthy Aging — Is There a Role for Libraries?
- Serving the "Gorgeous Mosaic"— Multicultural Collections and Programs: A Lesson in Why and How
- The Newest New Yorkers: Who Are They? Where Are They? Can We Serve Them Better?

Critical to sustaining these programs for the poor is the New York Public Library's commitment to acknowledging the dedication and hard work of the staff. The Mayer Stern Award, awarded yearly, has been given to the branch librarians at the West Farms, Hamilton Grange, Melrose and Morrisana branches, which primarily serve poor, minority and non–English-speaking populations. The Bertha Franklin Feder Award for Outstanding Service to Librarianship has been awarded to the Community Specialist for Staten Island Branches, the Community Specialist for Manhattan Branches, and the Supervising Librarian for CLASP (Connecting Libraries and School Projects), all of whom develop and implement programs in areas that serve the most disadvantaged New Yorkers. Staff who develop programs for the poor have also been acknowledged by the communities they serve and the city of New York by being awarded the Sloan Public Service Award by the Fund for the City of New York for exemplary contributions to the city.

The New York Public Library is constantly seeking ways to serve those who need library services the most. The Outreach Services Advisory Committee, comprised of community and government agency representatives and their clients, meets twice a year to review and evaluate current library service, to make suggestions for enhancing services and developing new services, and provide a forum for negotiating collaborations and joint sponsorship of programs. They have made suggestions regarding the placement of programs, the font size that should be used for flyers, the availability of community resources that complement library resources, and their availability to participate in staff sensitivity training. In addition, the Borough Community Specialists network on a regular basis with a variety of city-wide agencies and organizations to facilitate program development and implementation.

The words of students in the literacy program best answer the question, "Libraries and the Poor: What's the Connection?"

> I am writing to tell you that I am glad to come to school to better myself in reading and writing. I want to help myself. When I go to an agency I want to be able to fill out the application form. That will help me get a job and go for

my GED. I am not giving up because I know that God is with me and He will take care of things for me and give me the strength to carry on my work.

Ladies and gentlemen, I am glad to be here. This program means a lot to me. I want to thank all the tutors who take their time to teach us how to read and write. I would like to thank the director of this program. This program means a lot to people. When I was on a plane going to Washington D.C. someone was talking about this program. Six months ago I was not able to read a sentence. This is a true story. Thank you very much.

Notes

1. Joseph B. Rose, *Annual Report on Social Indicators* (New York: Dept. of City Planning, 1994, 1995, 1996).

2. Terry J. Rosenberg, *Poverty in New York City, 1993: An Update* (New York: Community Services Society of New York, 1994): 13.

3. Joseph B. Rose, *The Newest New Yorkers 1990–1994* (New York: Dept. of City Planning, 1996).

4. Steven Likosky, *Connections: A Guide for Ex-Inmates and the Job Search Guide* (New York: New York Public Library, 1997).

On-Site Library Centers

BY MARY D. TEASLEY
AND DELORIS WALKER-MOSES

The Newark (New Jersey) Public Library has always sought to provide services to special populations in the city, but discovered that it was not serving almost 35,000 residents who lived in public housing. According to Harold Lucas, executive director of the Newark Housing Authority,

> The need for special library services to public housing residents has long been documented, and several research studies have shown that public housing residents are often physically, economically and socially isolated from their surroundings and may not easily avail themselves of valuable services. Therefore, why not bring the library to the housing sites?[1]

Having reviewed some of the studies, and inspired by the Chicago Public Library project at the Robert Taylor Homes, the Newark Public Library applied for a special populations grant from the U.S. Department of Housing and Urban Development to collaborate with the Newark Housing Authority in establishing reading centers at five public housing sites. With the help of Newark's mayor Sharpe James, Rep. Donald Payne, and senators Frank Lautenberg and Bill Bradley, the library received a $500,000 grant award in 1992.

Alex Boyd, library director, politicians and community activists were enthusiastic about the opportunity to serve the public housing community. When Congressman Payne, a resident of Newark, announced the grant award, he said that "this housing authority-library project was unique, the best way to utilize each others' resources; it just makes sense to bring people who know how to deal with literacy and education together with people who deal with the quality of life."[2] We summarize our experiences here with the hope that the Newark project might serve as a model for others.

Background

The City of Newark was established in 1666 and is the largest in New Jersey. The 1990 U.S. Census counted 275,122 persons in the city, 58.5 percent of them of African American descent, 26.1 percent Hispanic, and 15.4 percent other ethnic groups . A profile of Newark's children produced from the 1990 U.S. Census data, compiled in 1996 by the Association for the Children of New Jersey, disclosed that 26.3 percent of the people in the city are below the U.S. poverty level, 41.4 percent of female-headed households are below the poverty level, and 37.2 percent of children live below poverty level. Data released from the Newark Public Schools on standardized test scores reveals that 24.9 percent of fourth grade students taking the "Stanford 8" failed reading, 32.4 percent of the eighth graders taking the "Early Warning Test" failed reading, and 39.4 percent of eleventh graders taking the "High School Proficiency Test" failed reading. The drop-out rate for Newark students was almost 10 percent in 1993. The need for educational initiatives is apparent when over 48 percent of residents have not achieved a high school diploma, and 20 percent are estimated to be functionally illiterate. The number of residents with incomes below the poverty rate is estimated at almost 30 percent.[3]

The city has yet to fully rebound from the riots of 1967, which resulted in the destruction of many homes and businesses. An escalating unemployment rate (estimated at nearly 14 percent in 1994) has especially affected the poor, who often lack the personal and technical skills demanded in a changing labor force, and lack access to personal transportation necessary for jobs in distant suburban areas. Because of its waterfront location, and its status as home to five colleges and universities and as a center for the arts (which includes the Newark Museum and the new $200 million New Jersey Performing Arts Center), Newark is experiencing a renaissance of economic and cultural activity.

The Newark Public Library, incorporated in 1888, is made up of the main library, which houses over 1.5 million volumes, and a branch system that includes ten sites throughout the city. The library serves as a resource to the entire state of New Jersey in particular collection areas. In addition to the city population, NPL serves almost 10,000 city commuters and college students. The library is proud to be known as "a people's university" and conducts numerous traditional and nontraditional outreach services to the city residents and the greater–Newark community, including the deaf, illiterate, immigrants, preschoolers, disabled, students, parents and the elderly.

The Newark Housing Authority (NHA), which falls under the federal Housing and Urban Development Agency, is the eighth largest in the nation. The Authority administers six large complexes and smaller sites throughout the city. According to Harry Robinson, director of public relations for the NHA, there are 8,935 units occupied by about 35,000 residents — which is over 12 percent of the city's population — with an average annual family income of $8200. Although in its original design, public housing was intended to be transitional, in its evolution it has become permanent housing for many, even multigenerational for some families. The NHA is proud of its accomplishments and the progressive measures it has taken to transform the quality of life for its residents. It has changed public housing by building 1,000 new townhouses in the last four years and scattered them throughout the city, and consequently has increased the market value of private real estate.

As we proceed to the actual steps taken to establish these centers, we will first summarize the all important grant proposal that financed this project, as it would illustrate better the goals and objectives, and help introduce what we, as site coordinators, were trying to accomplish

Grant Proposal

RATIONALE FOR THE ESTABLISHMENT OF CENTERS

- Over 12 percent of the city's population live in public housing
- This population is dramatically underserved
- The need and demand for informational, educational, leisure reading materials and literacy services is great among this population
- An effective "intervention" program would promote use of library services and enhance the lives of public housing residents

PROGRAM OBJECTIVES

- To educate public housing residents on how library resources can be used to improve or enhance their lives
- To raise the level of awareness and knowledge about the availability of library services and how to access these services
- To promote the use of the Newark Public Library branches and main library by public housing residents

- To introduce public housing residents to the "information super-highway" through computer training and use of electronic information resources
- To include literacy training and instruction for public housing residents

PROGRAM DESCRIPTION

Five small, self-contained, resident-managed library resource rooms were established to deliver services to specific resident populations within the NHA. One room was larger and designated as the "hub" site. The targeted breakdown follows: two were youth and family sites, two were senior citizen sites and one special site that targeted youthful, recovering substance abusers. Each site was remodeled, refurbished , and made serviceable and attractive.

LIBRARY COORDINATORS

Two Newark Public Library professional librarians served as coordinators. Their duties were to:

- work with residents at each site to determine specific needs
- contact vendors, order materials and equipment for the project
- organize the initial phase of programs and workshops
- supervise the installation of furniture, equipment and materials
- write reports, evaluations and recommendations
- train resident site managers at each host complex
- function as liaisons between the NPL and NHA administrators
- prepare site managers to handle the project after the NPL staff leaves

RESIDENT SITE MANAGERS

Five residents recommended by the Newark Housing Authority tenant groups served as resident library site managers. Their functions were to:
- plan and provide basic library and literacy services
- access NPL resources through TOPCAT (Newark's public access catalog)
- serve as liaisons between the centers and the Newark Public Library
- learn acquisition procedures and order materials
- plan and schedule programs and workshops
- arrange for resident transport to events.
- plan and execute literacy-tutoring and activities
- keep attendance records of reading center use and program activity
- submit monthly reports of all reading center use, and include any problems encountered and requests from residents

When we received this grant we had a two year time limit to establish these centers. From the beginning we began experiencing obstacles. We lost six months as numerous municipal resolutions had to be passed to accept the grant, incorporate it into the city's budget, and appoint a liaison to monitor the grant and disburse funds. Our next task was to locate five sites for the reading centers. In selecting the sites, we applied several criteria: (1) There must be strong need and demonstrated interest from the residents as well as effective tenant leaders who would facilitate the project; (2) there must be appropriate space available and a resident population that corresponded to the target populations specified in the grant; and (3) room size and geographical location must be appropriate. Although no site was "user-ready," there had to be a reasonable potentiality for use after modest remodeling and refurbishing.

The five sites and target populations selected were :

Baxter Terrace	Family/Senior Citizen Site
Bradley Court	Family Site
James C. White Manor	Senior Citizens
Seth Boyden Elderly	Senior Citizens
Soul-O-House	Youthful, Recovering Substance Abusers

Site Preparation

To bring these rooms into an acceptable condition, the library's architectural consultant mapped out the exact specifications and requirements for painting, replacing doors and windows, ceiling tiles and flooring, upgrading lighting and electrical capacity in order to accommodate air conditioning and computers. An important feature was that the reading centers had to be designed to be multipurpose rooms with a library environment. Therefore, the architect was asked to custom-design modular units that would house safely and securely the computers and other items vulnerable to theft. These units would serve as flip-down work tables which could be used for library activities, but would not interfere with other activities taking place in the same room. The actual renovation work was done by the staff of the Newark Housing Authority.

The site preparation was in process when we, as site coordinators, were brought into the project . As branch library managers, we had worked with numerous community groups and had experience in planning programs and implementing and coordinating grants. The initial work had been handled by the two project directors: Wilma Grey, assistant director for community library services at NPL, and Gloria Currey-Williams, assistant to the chief at NHA who had delineated a list of responsibilities connected with the establishment of these library resource/service centers. In order to complete the project on time, we were relieved of our regular NPL duties.

Training of Resident Site Managers

The initial challenge was to find responsive residents for the library site manager positions and begin to train them. Five were recommended by the tenant presidents of the host complexes. Training began with orientation, where the site managers were apprised of their duty to attend classes held in the main library at least twice a week. Instruction covered what public libraries are, what librarians do, how books are ordered, ISBN numbers, the Dewey Classification system, the purpose of the catalog, and basic library operations such as registration of users, circulation, shelving, filing, and record keeping. They received homework assignments and went on field trips which helped them to use their newly acquired skills and knowledge. (See example, Appendix A, at the end of this chapter.) They were amazed to see the massive collections and the computerized catalog we call TOPCAT. Because we wanted them to become familiar with the world of work, the training and learning atmosphere was relaxed but structured. They were exposed to activities planning, design and implementation of programs, and outreach techniques useful for introducing and involving residents in this project.

Training was rapid because we had to cover many aspects of library operations in a very short time. The grant provided the coordinators for professional support for 18 months but gradually during the last six months of this 24 month project, management responsibilities would shift to the NHA managers.

Only two of the resident site managers had any experience using libraries, and one of those had to be replaced because a substance abuse problem was not yet under control. Most site managers were fearful that they would not succeed, as this was more than they had thought would be required, but through perseverance and tenacity they did. One trainee questioned, "Do librarians do all this?" The training was a learning experience for the managers and a challenge for the coordinators.

Reading Room Collections and Equipment

We needed to identify the materials and equipment needed in each center. Needs assessment forms enabled the coordinators and site managers to "custom-design" each collection and gave insight into the type of programs and activities desired at each complex (see Senior User Needs Survey Form in Appendix B, at the end of this chapter). The NHA arranged for each family in the host complex to receive a form, which was to be returned to the complex manager's office, and placed in a beautifully decorated box marked LIBRARY. The library managers picked up the forms and followed-up at sites where response was low, tabulated the results, and provided this information to the site coordinators.

Many of the needs identified were specific to particular sites. At the senior sites — James C. White Manor and Seth Boyden Elderly — large print materials, magnifying sheets, educational games, books on cassette and videos were a priority, in addition to books on holiday activities, crafts, sewing, and cooking. Interest was expressed also in programming and talks about health, cooking for one or two, and living on a fixed income. Surprisingly, residents at these sites were very interested in having a children's collection available for use by their grandchildren. The children's collection remains a focal point of the main collection at both elderly sites.

The Essex Soul House Reading Center is a valuable resource for the residents in the Stella Wright complex, which is located in one of the poorest and most crime ridden areas of the city. The reading center is located in an on-site medical clinic called Soul-O-House. There were many requests for materials on health issues and diseases, and inspirational and life-skill materials, since this facility serves the medical needs of recovering addicts, administers medical tests for pregnancy, HIV and AIDS, and presents counseling services. Administrators requested materials to assist clients in understanding their illnesses and the accompanying problems they face. We invited and welcomed requests from each public housing resident. The families at Stella Wright Homes requested books on problem solving, career exploration, resume writing and teaching aids to assist students with homework.

At Bradley Court the residents are primarily nonworking, low-income, single-parent families, but there are a few working poor who have lived there almost all their lives. The primary focus here was on books and teaching aids that would help the children with homework assignments, and assist parents through materials on child rearing, health, GED and career materials, videos, and recreational reading, and life skills books for teens and young adults. There was great interest in computer software and electronic tools among the youth.

At the hub site, Baxter Terrace, requests focused on educational study guides, GED and career materials, child care, literacy materials, African American and Latino literature, citizenship guidebooks, health, games, large print materials, magnifiers, and much interest was expressed in programming and activities.

In addition to the specific materials requested by the various sites, the coordinators purchased a collection of educational software, CD-ROMs, print and electronic encyclopedias, literacy materials, videos, games, encyclopedias and other reference materials, periodicals, and ethnic and local newspapers for each center.

Literacy Tutor Training

Literacy programming and activities were a major component of the grant, as literacy is critical to becoming successful and self-sufficient. Activities that involved reading, writing, listening and speaking were primary to the planning process. Core literacy materials included books, self-teaching computer software, and audio and video aids for children and adults.

Because library managers were responsible for planning and handling literacy activities, each was required to attend the tutor-training program conducted by Literacy Volunteers of America, Inc. (LVA). This training of 18 to 21 hours was open to all interested public housing staff and residents and was held at NPL. The Literacy Volunteers employ the language-experience approach that uses the student's needs and personal experiences as a basis for instruction. Only four of the nine public housing residents who attended the sessions were certified but the others received valuable information that they can use advantageously. The NHA project director and the coordinators attended the sessions also and were certified as tutors. One of the first managers to begin tutoring was a senior citizen. The certifications were a great asset to the project and a benefit to the individual tutor.

Operating the Centers

When we first initiated this project, we encountered obstacles of resistance by tenant leaders and a few residents. The Marketing Institute survey conducted in 1988 for the Chicago Public Library alerted us to some of the sensitivities and social needs of public housing residents: the need for involvement of residents in decision making, the uniqueness of the service area, the extreme sensitivity of the residents to outside perceptions, and their isolation.[4] In one case a tenant president who believed that we were infringing upon her territory and usurping her power, summoned the Newark Tenants' Council. The dispute was quickly resolved but the incident made us more aware.

Another conflict resulted from the placement of library centers in multipurpose rooms. Some residents expressed concern that the library collection and equipment would require too much space. At one senior site, a wheelchair bound resident was happy for the reading rooms but inquired, "Where are we going to have our dances if they put books in that room?" As the residents began to watch the rooms being transformed through painting, carpeting, special alphabet rugs for the childrens' play area, color-coordinated furniture, 25-inch color televisions, VCRs, videos, audiocassettes, computers, and numerous new books arriving, they began to ask what could they do to help things along. Some residents expected the centers to be an extension of past experiences, which involved collections of donated, used, out-dated books. Additional interest was aroused as parents realized that their children could obtain information in the environs of the housing complex, eliminating some hazards encountered traveling to the main library or a branch; that they could experience recreational activities and receive computer training on state-of-the-art equipment; and that all programs and resources were accessible on the complex surroundings. The interest that had been generated was now turning residents toward active involvement in establishing the reading centers.

Official Opening of the Centers

The site managers worked hard to prepare their rooms and compiled lists of VIPs to be invited to the grand opening for all the centers, which were officially named the Newark Housing Authority Reading Centers. On April 4, 1994, the grand opening was held at the hub site, Baxter Terrace, and attended by about 300 city politicians, community representatives, NPL and NHA administrators and staff, the very proud public housing residents, and friends. A video presentation of activities being conducted at each of the five sites was shown to the group: spelling bees, homework assistance and tutoring groups, electronic and board games, drama groups, bingo, chess, computer activities, and craft sessions. The guests were amazed to see that we had established state-of-the-art reading centers in all five public housing sites, not just the hub site. They were impressed by the flurry of activity among the resident participants.

Impact of Reading Centers

It has been four years since the opening of the NHA Reading Centers. While involved in the project, we saw many lives influenced by the reading centers and received many accolades for our efforts.

One of the two part-time managers at Baxter Terrace Reading Center, Venus Baskerville, said that the reading center at that site had filled a great need. She said that there is a high drop-out rate among the youth and many others are at risk because of poor basic skills, especially literacy; many parents have low literacy skills and try to hide it, but they send their children to the reading center for help. She reported that she had trained four children to read and helped many others enhance their literacy skills. One six year old was trying to learn to read but had never learned his alphabet. Three other children through social promotion were in the fourth or fifth grade and didn't know how to read. Having a library site with literacy tutoring services so accessible was a boon to them. Children came daily for homework assistance and recreational activities, and according to Baskerville, just for a little attention or to have someone to talk to about their problems. Some children have a very neglectful and disturbing home life, resulting in low self-esteem. "The library room is like a home to them," Baskerville said, " a place where they can feel welcome. I often had to put them out at closing. "

The efforts of the site managers at Baxter Terrace were noticed by the local school. One teacher wrote the tenant president and asked for permission to bring classes from the school to introduce the students to the reading centers, since most lived in the Baxter complex, and the grades of those who used the library had improved immensely. An on-site preschool group and day camp also visited the library for activities and programs. Senior citizens at the site enjoyed attending programs and watching the youth perform. Definitely the quality of life for all the residents who use the library collection or its services has been improved. Even those who do not utilize the services are very proud to have such a facility with the resources on site.

Both reading center managers at the Baxter Terrace site are being replaced, as they have just been assigned to full-time positions with NHA. Working in the reading center allowed them to upgrade their skills and move up the economic ladder. The increase in salary has allowed one of them to move into traditional housing and both to become self-sufficient.

Bradley Court Reading Center occupies a very special place in its community. This site was used for local girl scout council meetings for the entire year. Few places in the area have attractively decorated rooms to accommodate such groups and which are useful for local events. In addition to the students coming into the center for homework assistance and recreational activities, there is an adult group called "Sisterhood" that was started by the reading center manager, Darice Fogg. This group focuses on self-enhancement techniques through literacy training, "sharing" of information about womanhood and family life, and recommended readings on subjects discussed. This is an example of a resident helping other residents to see themselves as capable of making significant contributions to their children, family, and community while promoting the importance of knowledge in that quest. Darice is a college student who continues to live in public housing, as her income is inadequate for tuition and traditional housing. While she remains a resident, she desires to make a contribution to the welfare of the resident population at Bradley Court.

Seth Boyden Elderly Reading Center is a site located on the outskirts of a large family complex. Although this is designated as a senior site, ever since its opening the children and adults from the family units have been coming to the reading center for resources for school work or recreational reading and, of course, all public housing residents are allowed to use the center. The seniors are very proud of their center and come daily for reading materials, activities, social interaction, and often for information for debating purposes.

Programming at Seth Boyden allowed us to discover some of the special talents and valuable skills of the residents. Most were bashful initially when we asked them to participate in the programs but after one resident volunteered, poets, singers and storytellers in the midst emerged. A retired school aide was encouraged to share her skills and trains residents in computer literacy, and a retired minister conducts arts and crafts sessions. In addition to programming, each of the sites has large holiday celebrations such as Christmas and Kwanzaa that allow residents to meet each other and also to become familiar with the reading center resources and programs.

The James C. White Manor Reading Center is a high-rise elderly site containing 206 units. The reading center is used also for meetings and church services. It has a large-print collection and cassette players that circulate, which allows many of the residents to enjoy books on tape and audiocassettes. Videos are extremely popular and are used for programs in the Community Room. Also, the reading center conducts a " how-to-do-it" club twice a month for those desiring to learn to crochet and sew.

Residents were extremely proud to receive a visitation from a group of public housing officials from Russia, where they could show off their "fully-equipped" reading center.

Essex Soul House (Soul-O-House) of Stella Wright Homes is located on the largest of the family sites of 808 units. Although it is a clinic for recovering substance abusers and HIV, pregnancy and AIDS screenings, it is also located in one of the most crime-ridden and drug infested areas of the city. There was definitely a great need for a center here.

The clinic users have access to additional information on their diseases and inspirational books and videos to encourage and support them in life-threatening situations. Very young children and students are able to find colorful picture books or textbooks with characters identifiable with their own ethnic and racial group as well as information. Parents and the many latchkey children are grateful for a "safe haven" that protects and assists them in their education.

The Soul-O-House site managers are certified LVA tutors and are very actively involved in tutoring many children who have benefited from this service. Literacy and mathematics software was of great use and help to the children and their parents.

Conclusion

This project was one of the biggest challenges but greatest rewards for us and the Newark Public Library. It was definitely much larger than it appeared on paper. The NHA Reading Centers are definitely a feasible project and visible symbol of progress in the public housing community.

We learned many lessons about public housing and the information needs and desires of the residents. The public housing community, which has been labeled "hard to reach," allowed us to come into *their* communities, and worked with us to implement a project that would enhance their quality of life. Their response has been overwhelmingly very positive and they continue to maintain these reading rooms and express a desire for more to be placed throughout the city.

Although we were not able to evaluate this endeavor as desired due to timelines for our participation, an interview with Gloria Currey-Williams, NHA project director, revealed that the reading centers are actively used and approximately 30 to 50 residents visit the family sites daily for research, homework assistance and tutoring. Many have learned to read or are reading better and have developed an interest in learning and libraries. The reading centers on the elderly sites are the central meeting spot for resources, activities, programs or just socializing. Many have become computer literate and student grades are improving.

As we analyze this project and evaluate some of the NPL/NHA

initiatives, we are pleased to enumerate some of the achievements and accomplishments and the services that were available:

- Residents became familiar with library resources and services
- Residents were able to enhance basic education skills and acquire knowledge
- Career development and job seeking guides were distributed
- Reading Center users learned better information seeking skills
- Computer literacy training was conducted
- Literacy tutoring and skills training was given
- Homework assistance for students was provided
- Custom-designed reading center collections were provided
- The programs afforded employment opportunities for housing residents

We are most pleased to have participated in this project. For many the burden of illiteracy was lessened and some parents are now better equipped to take care of their children. Some are more knowledgeable of their heritage and are more familiar with life outside the complex. These centers have become "gatekeepers" within the public housing community and "gateways" to the mainstream and a life of self-sufficiency for many. Although this project was experimental, its success has generated interest and inquiry throughout the United States.

APPENDIX A.
HOMEWORK ASSIGNMENT

For All Site Managers:
Assignment due: 2/22/94

Visit Your Library Site and Assess the Site. Describe It as Follows:

1. **Size:** Lighting, number of doors, entrances and exits, bulletin board space, number of tables and chairs, electrical outlets, windows, heating and/or air conditioning units, etc.

2. **Do you foresee any problems?** With what areas? Why?

3. **What, if anything, has been done at the site?** Is it being renovated? Have renovations been completed? Has nothing been done? (Include stage of renovation.)

4. **What needs to be done?** (If anything)

5. **Name the kinds (types) of materials you think will be needed.** (Be specific)

6. **What kind of equipment is needed?** Games? Services?

7. **Is the library space being used now?** By whom? For what? How often?

8. **Explain why you think that the library will be beneficial for the residents.** Add any additional insight about your library site.

APPENDIX B.
USER NEEDS SURVEY
FOR THE SENIOR LIBRARY CENTER
AT THE JAMES C. WHITE MANOR

Please help us assess the information needs of the residents in this complex by completing the questionnaire and returning it to the Manager's Office by March 11, 1994. Your input is valuable.

1. A senior Library center will be located at the James C. White Manor. Do you think that you will use the library? Yes _____ No _____

2. Would you most often use the materials in the library center

a. for pleasure? _____

b. to become a better reader? _____

c. to increase your knowledge of certain subjects? _____

d. to learn practical life skills? _____

e. to learn to solve personal or family problems? _____

f. other _____

3. What kinds of library materials would you find most useful to have in the library center?

a. books _____   g. videocassettes _____

b. magazines _____   h. computers _____

c. large print materials _____   i. typewriters _____

d. magnifying devices _____   j. newspapers _____

e. books on tape _____   k. music _____

f. audiocassettes _____   l. other _____

4. Check the topics that would be of interest to you.

a. inspirational and religious _____   g. health _____

b. famous people _____   h. nutrition _____

c. personal finance _____   i. cooking _____

d. vacations and travel _____   j. poetry _____

e. hobbies and crafts _____   k. black studies _____

f. mystery stories _____   l. Other _____

5. What kinds of programs would you be interested in attending in the library center?

a. talks/discussions _____

b. film/video _____

c. musical programs _____

d. workshops _____

e. other _____

6. Do you have any suggestions for speakers or entertainers or topics that you would like included in the library center programs? (Please list them below.)

(If you need any help filling out this form, please contact the complex managers office.)

Notes

1. Terry P. Guess, "U.S. Grant to Let Newark Library Establish Satellites at Housing Complexes," *The Star Ledger* (March 30, 1993): 54.

2. *Ibid.*

3. "Newark Kids Count: A Profile of Child Well-Being," prepared by the Association for Children of New Jersey, 1996.

4. Deborah J. Spiller and Michael Baker, "Library Service to Residents of Public Housing Developments: A Study and Commentary," *Public Libraries* 28 (Nov./Dec. 1989): 358–61.

RURAL
POVERTY PROGRAMS

Library Services
to Farm Workers in
West Central Florida

BY KATHLEEN DE LA PEÑA MCCOOK
AND KATE LIPPINCOTT

The coexistence of extreme poverty and comfortable affluence in west central Florida presents a wrenching challenge to librarians: how to develop collections and services to meet the needs of all people. While this is a central tenet of library service, it does not happen easily.

The poor in west central Florida are a shadow presence. They are not counted in the census and they cannot make use of governmental services. These poor are farm workers — many migratory and many undocumented. Migrant farm workers sustain Florida's agricultural economy, which is second only to tourism in its importance to Florida's economy. Florida's leading crops are citrus, landscape foliage, tomatoes, strawberries and cane/sugar. Harvesting these crops is a grueling task, requiring farm laborers to spend long hours bent over in the fields in Florida's hot, steamy climate.

Public libraries in west central Florida have tried to develop services for farm workers, but in some agricultural counties a single librarian oversees public library services to all people, and the level of outreach needed to serve farm workers can not be developed effectively. Nevertheless, Florida librarians have continued their efforts in this regard.

Sometimes action begins from very small seeds. As director of the library science program at the University of South Florida in Tampa, Kathleen de la Peña McCook began making site visits to many libraries in the region in 1993. Easily confused by state roads and county roads with the same number, she often found herself far out in citrus groves or tomato fields. These groves and fields were filled with farm workers and their families picking oranges, tomatoes and peppers. Trying to determine the extent to which these workers were served by the region's public libraries, she and Kate Lippincott decided to survey libraries in the region.

The desire to address the needs of the unserved has been central to the profession since its inception. The outpouring of effort to accomplish this goal in the 1960s and 1970s (documented by Weibel) manifested itself in many library-based projects, some of which were allied with programs of library and information science education.[1]

The great dividing line, so coincidental with the millennium, has been drawn by digitization and the Internet. The recent focus for many schools that educate librarians has been, of perceived necessity, on technological competence. The word library has even been banished from the names of many schools that once focused proudly on the education of librarians. Yet the iconographic status of the word holds resonance we should not abandon.

The time and financial costs of analyzing the needs of the poor through survey research were justified by the core values held by the faculty of the School of Library and Information Science. The faculty of the school have determined that work on issues of community outreach is an essential component of their teaching, service and research.

Tampa Bay Library Consortium

Florida's libraries are organized into six multi-type library cooperatives devoted to sharing resources among all libraries. The multi-type cooperative that functions in west central Florida is the Tampa Bay Library Consortium (TBLC). The twelve counties served by this Consortium are Citrus, Desoto, Hardee, Hernando, Highlands, Hillsborough, Manatee, Okeechobee, Pasco, Pinellas, Polk and Sarasota. The range of public library support is extreme, as shown in Table 1.

Table 1. Per Capita Library Funding
in the Tampa Bay Library Consortium
Ranked Highest to Lowest for 1994/95

TBLC Counties	A. Per Capita 1994/95[2]	A. Per Capita 1992/93[3]	A. Population B. 1994 (estimated)[4]
Hillsborough	16.81	13.81	879,069
Pinellas	16.34	12.98	870,722
Sarasota	16.11	12.81	296,002
Citrus	15.00	13.90	102,846
Hernando	13.98	11.58	114,866
Manatee	12.91	12.12	228,283
Pasco	12.27	13.95	298,852
Highlands	7.42	5.78	75,860
Hardee	5.44	4.24	22,454
Okeechobee	5.16	4.83	32,325
Desoto	4.70	4.90	26,260
Polk[5]			437,204

National Average per Capita Funding for Public Libraries in 1993 — $19.16[6]

TBLC counties have per capita library support ranging from $4.70 to $16.81— bare-bones funding (with all counties below the national average) that doesn't permit librarians to focus on outreach or services to special populations. Amidst a library funding environment that provides traditional services including access to the Internet, it has been difficult for libraries to focus attention and scarce resources on outreach.

Florida, overall an affluent state, ranks low in support for schools and libraries in large part because wealthy retired people flock to the state and determinedly fight taxes. The popular image of Florida as a sun-soaked region with miles of beaches, where the well-to-do retired live in gleaming condominiums, is a reality only for those who live on the Atlantic east of interstate 95, or along the Gulf west of interstate 75, or south of interstate 10.[7]

The counties of west central Florida that make up the TBLC area demonstrate a striking juxtaposition of wealth and poverty. Along the glittering coast of Sarasota's Long Boat Key north through St. Petersburg and Clearwater across the expanse of Tampa Bay, yachts and high rises claim the beaches, the water and the view. The workers that service this economy live in mobile homes east of the interstate among scrub palmetto and mined-out phosphate pits. Produce stands tended by families abound. The meager profits from these marginal enterprises pay for a car bought at numerous "NO CREDIT NEEDED, YOUR JOB IS YOUR CREDIT" roadside outlets.

The sail boaters, jet skiers and snowbirds fleeing winter cluster along the coasts or flock together in gated, deed-restricted communities. The interior of the state, with the exception of Disneyworld, is a vast agricultural fruit and vegetable region. Sarasota County on the Gulf coast has a per capita income of $28,761; Okeechobee County, which is inland to the East, has a per capita income of $14,227.

Poverty is not a static concept. Statisticians and demographers struggle to delineate income levels that define poverty, but the variables that must be considered defy clarity. Perhaps nowhere is this problem of definition more difficult than west central Florida. Living conditions of the rich and poor are at once a jumble and a fearful segregation. The shores are patrolled by sentinel condominiums costing astronomical sums for a gulf or ocean view. A typical rental of $3000 a month on the Gulf contrasts with a mobile home rent of $127 a month just a few miles to the East.

TABLE 2. TBLC COUNTIES PERSONAL INCOME
PER CAPITA RANKED FROM HIGHEST TO LOWEST

TBLC Counties	Per Capita Income 1995[8]	% Below Poverty Level 1995[9]
Sarasota	28,761	7%
Pinellas	22,798	10%
Manatee	21,584	10%
Hillsborough	19,129	13%
Polk	16,858	13%
Highlands	16,541	15%
Hardee	15,490	23%
Citrus	15,295	13%
Hernando	15,251	11%
Pasco	15,176	12%
Desoto	15,043	19%
Okeechobee	14,227	21%

National Average Personal Income per Capita in 1995 — 22,788
Florida Average Personal Income per Capita in 1995 — 22,916, ranked 20th in nation[10]

For a variety of reasons, Florida, ranked the twentieth most affluent state in the nation, consistently supports schools and libraries near the low level of personal income. It ranked thirty-sixth in support of education and forty-ninth in the number of public libraries and branches per 10,000 population.[11] Ironically, one large retirement community sits between two agricultural areas. Migrant workers labor at yard work, trimming the golf course-quality lawns, but they and their children are not permitted to use the pools or private library.

The working poor who service the condominiums and luxury hotels of the oceanside dwellers, as well as the farm workers who live nearby, are easily overlooked. Winter visitors fly directly to their resorts, or speed down the interstate highways that connect to causeways over glittering azure waters and elevate to grand views from which the fragile mobile home parks cannot even be seen.

Describing the Migrant Farm Worker Community

Who are those that make up the migrant farm worker community of Florida? According to Carlos Saavedra, the director of the Florida Department of Education's Adult Migrant Education Program, they are 70 to 80 percent native-born Americans primarily of Mexican descent, not recent immigrants. They move around in the U.S. from state to state or within the state. Saavedra's statistics show that the average family income is $7,500 and that families have an average of five children. Their educational attainments and language levels are very low. The estimates on the number of migrant farm workers vary widely according to the source, and most sources are considerably out of date. The U.S. Department of Health and Human Services estimated from surveys performed in the late 1980s that there were about 56,245 migrant workers and their families in the TBLC area.[12] Florida as a whole is estimated to have between 183,000 to 400,000 migrant farm workers and ranks third behind California and Texas.

The relationship between poverty and living conditions (rather than an income below the official poverty line) is explored by Federman et al.[13] Their analysis of nine representative surveys on the living conditions of the poor identify factors that bear consideration by librarians. Poor children are more likely to:

- repeat a grade;
- drop out of school;
- have less access to computers at home or school;
- watch more television;
- have fewer books at home.

These factors form an "index of deprivation" and a blueprint for librarians who want to address the needs of the poor.

On the edge of the Everglades in Collier County southeast of the TBLC area, Immokalee is home to about 20,000 migrant farm workers. The Immokalee Branch of the Collier County Library System began designing special programs and services for the farm workers and their families in 1993. Recognizing that basic transportation to the library was a significant obstacle, the library made a concerted effort to focus on outreach services that would bring library services to the people. The library also began changing the shape of its collection by selecting more materials in Spanish and more materials that would directly appeal to the needs of this special population. This example of a library working cooperatively and creatively with the community and with existing service agencies serves as an inspiring example for librarians throughout the state.[14]

Task Force

The Tampa Bay Library Consortium's Migrant Worker Family Project Committee, initiated by faculty at the University of South Florida School of Library and Information Science, began in June 1996 as a task force of Florida librarians, educators, administrators, and students with a shared interest in initiating and expanding library services to the large migrant farm worker community in west central Florida. The Tampa Bay Library Consortium, founded in 1979, is a nonprofit multi-type library cooperative of libraries in a twelve-county area surrounding Tampa Bay. These counties range from heavily urban areas on the coast to very rural areas inland. TBLC membership is made up of eighty-three libraries including community college, private academic college and university, public school, public, and special libraries.[15] The consortium collaborates and cooperates on a range of resource-sharing projects from literacy to Internet access.

Addressing the needs of migrant farm workers and their families is an appropriate, worthwhile and necessary project for the consortium's constituents. Derrie Roark Perez, the 1996-97 TBLC president, emphasized that during her term TBLC would "stress people, our library staffs and our library patrons/clients/guests, with a two-pronged approach: 1) to stress the human needs of served and unserved populations and 2) to consider areas needing attention within our own ranks to help our staffs transition to the year 2000."[16] Taking Dr. Perez's emphasis as a mandate, TBLC's Board of Directors approved the Task Force as an official project.

As is typical in other parts of the country, the migrant farm workers tend to live in remote, isolated areas, often beyond the reach of many community programs and services that might benefit them, including library services. It was no surprise when the February 1996 survey of librarians in the TBLC area revealed that the migrant farm worker community was seen as a rather vague entity and that library services designed for them were few in number.[17]

This preliminary survey of all public libraries in the Tampa Bay Library Consortium was conducted by the University of South Florida School of Library and Information Research Group. The survey asked the librarians what services they were currently providing for this particular population. It was immediately clear from the results of the survey that little organized activity was taking place, beyond nominal Spanish-language collections, and that libraries had few materials that might meet the needs of migrant farm workers and their families. It was also clear that librarians were interested in the question and realized that their collections were weak in this area.

The survey asked for estimates of the numbers of migrant workers in the librarians' service areas. The answers to this question revealed the essential difficulty in getting any concrete figures. Census figures do not count migrant farm workers, as such. They count Spanish-speaking persons and farm laborers, but not as a combined unit. All survey participants agreed that regardless of the official count, there are large numbers of often invisible migrant farm workers working in different parts of the TBLC area at different times of the year.

Identification of Issues

Libraries were asked to list names of anyone who might be interested in meeting and discussing the issues, and the initial committee's membership was formed from that group. The organizational meeting of the Migrant Worker Family Project Committee (June 10, 1996, held in Wauchula at the Hardee County Public Library) focused on literacy. The majority of migrant farm workers and their families, though born and educated in the U.S., speak Spanish and are functionally illiterate in their native language, as well as English. An established goal of public libraries has been to assist in increasing literacy, which in the U.S. usually means English literacy. This becomes a far more complicated and confusing issue when an important question is introduced: can someone become literate in a second language when they are not yet literate in their first language? "Limited English proficiency is the single most important obstacle to upward mobility among Mexican immigrants," said Wayne Cornelius, the director of the Center for U.S. Mexican Studies at the University of California at San Diego.[18]

Several literacy coordinators were in attendance at that meeting, and a wide range of programs and theories were discussed. Though the meeting may have begun with the assumption that migrant workers and their families would be enticed into the library to increase their English language skills and general education level, it ended with the realization that more Spanish language materials — reference, easy-reading and children's — were a fundamental need. In conjunction with this was the frustration expressed by librarians in several smaller libraries, that when Spanish-speaking patrons do come into the library and require assistance, there are few Spanish-speaking librarians on the staff to assist them. This in turn brought up the obvious difficulty these same non–Spanish speaking librarians face in developing good Spanish language collections.

Spanish Language Materials List

A productive result of the first meeting was a project headed by Nelida Miranda, acquisitions librarian at the Tampa–Hillsborough County Public Library, to produce a list of the Spanish language materials in the Tampa–Hillsborough County Public Library's collection. Since this library's collection is substantial and growing, it was thought that a list could serve both as a guide for those involved in collection development in other libraries and as a way for non–Spanish speaking librarians to assist Spanish-speaking patrons in finding materials that might be useful to them. The list, titled *Spanish Language Materials in the Tampa–Hillsborough County Public Library System*, a collaborative project of the University of South Florida, the Tampa Bay Library Consortium and the Tampa–Hillsborough County Public Library, was published in February 1997 and made available to libraries in the TBLC service area.[19]

Continuing Dialogue

Carlos Saavedra, director of the Florida State Department of Education's Adult Migrant Program and Services Office, was guest speaker at the July 1996 meeting in the Bruton Memorial Library in Plant City. The program he administers provides training and supportive services necessary for unemployed farm workers to be able to obtain a full-time, year-round unsubsidized job. He vividly brought to light the realities of the life of the migrant farm worker, the worker's family, and migrants' most pressing needs. Mr. Saavedra's frank question to the Task Force — "Why would an illiterate migrant worker be interested in coming to a library?" — focused the discussion on the very real services that libraries can and do provide. His close experience with migrant workers helped to clarify how these services might be better shaped to meet the farm worker's actual needs. The two very different perspectives provided the spark for a mutually enlightening exchange of ideas and plans for collaborations in the future.

Techniques for selecting Spanish language materials were shared at a workshop in October 1996 conducted by special guest Linda Goodman of the Bilingual Publications Company of New York and Nelida Miranda of the Tampa–Hillsborough County Public Library. This type of meeting with a practical focus — i.e. providing hands-on experience — received enthusiastic responses from participants.

The Hugh Embry Branch Library in Dade City was the host site for the February 1997 meeting. Three local women — Carmen Meza of the Pasco Adult Migrant Program, Margarita Romo of Farm Workers Self Help, and Alicia Vega, a dropout counselor and representative of Unidos, all very involved with working with migrant farm workers and the Spanish-speaking community — discussed their perspectives on migrant farm workers and their needs. They brought increased attention to practical methods of reaching this population, such as the local radio stations, community centers, health centers, unofficial local gathering places and churches. This meeting continued the dialogue started by Mr. Saavedra between librarians and contacts in the field on the real needs of farm workers and how libraries can better serve them.

Statewide Concern

An exciting outgrowth of the interest in the Migrant Worker Family Project Committee of TBLC has been the establishment of a Florida Library Association discussion group called "Library Service to the Spanish Speaking," which was petitioned for by members of the TBLC Task Force. The first meeting of the discussion group was at the Florida Library Association's Annual Meeting in May 1997 in Daytona Beach. Linda Grisham, also of the Florida State Department of Education's Adult Migrant Program and Services Office, spoke to the group of librarians from around the state. Also speaking was Elizabeth Martinez, executive director of the American Library Association. After the meeting Martinez expressed great interest in supporting the connection between libraries and service agencies such as the Adult Migrant Education Program.

Grisham's presentation was designed to show the stark reality of everyday life for migrant farm workers and their families — the overcrowded and inadequate housing, the health and safety concerns, the educational inequities. A more subtle point she made, however, was that migrant farm workers are hardworking individuals who hope for a better life for themselves and their families. She emphasized that libraries must provide programs and services that would appeal and be of practical use to migrant farm workers. She suggested job and housing information as especially important, along with basic how-to information on social security cards, voter registration, car repair, and the like. Of interest to Grisham were the comments of the librarians in attendance, who described the many services and information sources that libraries already provide that might be useful to migrant workers and their families, such as meeting rooms and government information. This statewide effort to improve and expand library service to the Spanish speaking reflects the library profession's awareness of changing demographic trends and its strong commitment to serving all members of the community equally.

Projects for the Future

The work of the TBLC Migrant Worker Family Project Committee and the establishment of the Florida Library Association discussion group have created a strong network of committed librarians and developed a base of information and resources on which to build. Using the work of these groups as a foundation, Drs. Marilyn Stauffer and Derrie Roark Perez, professors at the University of South Florida School of Library and Information Science, were recently awarded an HEA Title II-B grant to present a week-long institute on Library Service to Migrant and Seasonal Farm Workers in the summer of 1998 for librarians. This institute will be a major stepping stone to increased and expanded service to migrant farm workers in Florida.

The Power of Committed Librarians

In this essay we have outlined how dozens of librarians have come together to define the need for service to the poor, gathered baseline data, developed fundamental resources, and planned a series of continuing education activities. During 1998 these west central Florida librarians will work together to produce Spanish language library public relations tools, including handouts and signs, and learn Spanish for library service. When convened, the 1998 University of South Florida School of Library and Information Science Library Service to Migrant and Seasonal Farm workers Institute will provide a culminating event in ongoing efforts to serve the unserved.

Notes

1. Kathleen Weibel, *The Evolution of Library Outreach 1960–75 and Its Effect on Reader Services: Some Considerations* (Occasional Papers Number 156, December 1982) (Urbana-Champaign, IL: University of Illinois, Graduate School of Library and Information Science, 1982).

2. *1996 Florida Library Directory with Statistics* (Tallahassee FL: Dept. of State, Division of Library Services, 1996): 152–153.

3. *1994 Florida Library Directory with Statistics* (Tallahassee FL: Dept. of State, Division of Library Services, 1994): 168–170.

4. Louise L. Hornor, Ed., *Florida Municipal Profiles 1995–96* (Palo Alto CA: Information Publications, 1995): 399–469.

5. Polk County's 13 municipal libraries cannot be combined for comparison.

6. *The Bowker Annual of Library and Book Trade Information*, 42nd ed. (New Providence NJ: Bowker, 1997): 430.

7. Of late the "I-4" corridor connecting Tampa, the Disney attractions, Orlando and Daytona along Interstate 4 has also become a swath of prosperity funded by tourism.

8. Del Marth, ed., *1997 Florida Almanac*, 13th ed. (Branford FL: Suwannee River): 176, 242.

9. *Ibid.*

10. *Statistical Abstract of the U.S., 1996* (Washington DC: U.S. Dept. of Commerce, Bureau of the Census, 1996): 453.

11. *State Rankings 1994; A Statistical View of the 50 United States* (Lawrence KS: Morgan Quitno, 1994): 129, 147.

12. *Migrant Health Program: An Atlas of State Profiles Which Estimate Number of Migrant and Seasonal Farmworkers and Members of Their Families* (Rockville, MD: U.S. Dept. of Health and Human Services, Public Health Service, March 1990): 44–46.

13. Maya Federman et al., "What Does It Mean to Be Poor in America," *Monthly Labor Review* 119 (May 1996).

14. Kathleen de la Peña McCook and Paula Geist, "Hispanic Library Services in South Florida," *Public Libraries* 34 (January/February 1995): 34–37.

15. Tampa Bay Library Consortium, *TBLC 1996/1997 Factsheet* (Tampa FL: TBLC, 1996).

16. Tampa Bay Library Consortium, "A Few Words from the President-Elect," *The TBLC News & Workshop Schedule* 5 (December 1996): 1.

17. Kate Lippincott, "Reaching Out to an Unserved Clientele: The TBLC Migrant Worker Family Project Committee," *Florida Libraries* 40 (June 1997): 73.

18. Carey Goldberg, "Hispanic Households Struggle Amidst Broad Decline in Income," *New York Times* (1/30/97): A-1.

19. Sonia Wohlmuth, ed., *Spanish Language Materials in the Tampa–Hillsborough County Public Library System: A List of Fiction Holdings by Author and a List of Non-Fiction Holdings by Subject Classification* (Tampa FL: Tampa Bay Library Consortium, 1997).

Appendix A:
Library Services for the Poor

APPROVED BY ALA IN JUNE 1990

The American Library Association promotes equal access to information for all persons, and recognizes the urgent need to respond to the increasing number of poor children, adults, and families in America. These people are affected by a combination of limitations, including illiteracy, illness, social isolation, homelessness, hunger, and discrimination, which hamper the effectiveness of traditional library services. Therefore, it is crucial that libraries recognize their role in enabling poor people to participate fully in a democratic society, by utilizing a wide variety of available resources and strategies. Concrete programs of training and development are needed to sensitize and prepare library staff to identify poor people's needs and deliver relevant services. And within the American Library Association the coordinating mechanisms for programs and activities dealing with poor people in various divisions, offices, and units should be strengthened, and support for low-income liaison activities should be enhanced.

Policy Objectives

The American Library Association shall implement these objectives by:

1. Promoting the removal of all barriers to library and information services, particularly fees and overdue charges.
2. Promoting the publication, production, purchase, and ready accessibility of print and nonprint materials that honestly address the issues of poverty and homelessness, that deal with poor people in a respectful way, and that are of practical use to low-income patrons.

165

3. Promoting full, stable, and ongoing funding for existing legislation programs in support of low-income services, and for pro-active library programs that reach beyond traditional service-sites to poor children, adults, and families.
4. Promoting training opportunities for librarians, in order to teach effective techniques for generating public funding to upgrade library services to poor people.
5. Promoting the incorporation of low-income programs and services into regular library budgets in all types of libraries, rather than the tendency to support these projects solely with "soft money" like private or federal grants.
6. Promoting equity in funding adequate library services for poor people in terms of materials, facilities, and equipment.
7. Promoting supplemental support for library resources for and about low-income populations by urging local, state, and federal governments, and the private sector, to provide adequate funding.
8. Promoting increased public awareness — through programs, displays, bibliographies, and publicity — of the importance of poverty-related library resources and services in all segments of society.
9. Promoting the determination of output measures through the encouragement of community needs assessments, giving special emphasis to assessing the needs of low-income people and involving both anti-poverty advocates and poor people themselves in such assessments.
10. Promoting direct representation of poor people and anti-poverty advocates through appointment to local boards and creation of local advisory committees on service to low-income people, such appointments to include library-paid transportation and stipends.
11. Promoting training to sensitize library staff to issues affecting poor people and to attitudinal and other barriers that hinder poor people's use of libraries.
12. Promoting networking and cooperation between libraries and other agencies, organizations, and advocacy groups in order to develop programs and services that effectively reach poor people.
13. Promoting the implementation of an expanded federal low-income housing program, national health insurance, full-employment policy; living minimum wage and welfare payments, affordable day care, and programs likely to reduce, if not eliminate, poverty itself.
14. Promoting among library staff the collection of food and clothing donations, volunteering personal time to anti-poverty activities and contributing money to direct-aid organizations.
15. Promoting related efforts concerning minorities and women, since these groups are disproportionately represented among poor people.

ALA Handbook of Organization 1995/1996

Appendix B:
Economic Barriers to Information Access

An Interpretation of the Library Bill of Rights

A democracy presupposes an informed citizenry. The First Amendment mandates the right of all persons to free expression, and the corollary right to receive the constitutionally protected expression of others. The publicly supported library provides free and equal access to information for all people of the community the library serves. While the roles, goals and objectives of publicly supported libraries may differ, they share this common mission.

The library's essential mission must remain the first consideration for librarians and governing bodies faced with economic pressures and competition for funding.

In support of this mission, the American Library Association has enumerated certain principles of library services in the LIBRARY BILL OF RIGHTS.

Principles Governing Fines, Fees and User Charges

Article I of the LIBRARY BILL OF RIGHTS states: "A person's right to use a library should not be denied or abridged because of origin, age, background, or views."

The American Library Association opposes the charging of user fees for the provision of information by all libraries and information services that

167

receive their major support from public funds. All information resources that are provided directly or indirectly by the library, regardless of technology, format, or methods of delivery, should be readily, equally and equitably accessible to all library users.

Libraries that adhere to these principles systematically monitor their programs of services for potential barriers to access and strive to eliminate such barriers when they occur. All library policies and procedures, particularly those involving fines, fees, or other user charges, should be scrutinized for potential barriers to access. All services should be designed and implemented with care, so as not to infringe on or interfere with the provision or delivery of information and resources for all users. Services should be re-evaluated on a regular basis to ensure that the library's basic mission remains uncompromised.

Librarians and governing bodies should look for alternative models and methods of library administration that minimize distinctions among users based on their economic status or financial condition. They should resist the temptation to impose users fees to alleviate financial pressures, at long term cost to institutional integrity and public confidence in libraries.

Library services that involved the provision of information, regardless of format, technology, or method of delivery, should be made available to all library users on an equal and equitable basis. Charging fees for the use of library collections, services, programs, or facilities that were purchased with public funds raises barriers to access. Such fees effectively abridge or deny access for some members of the community because they reinforce distinctions among users based on their ability and willingness to pay.

PRINCIPLES GOVERNING
CONDITIONS OF FUNDING

Article II of the LIBRARY BILL OF RIGHTS states: "Materials should not be proscribed or removed because of partisan or doctrinal disapproval."

Article III of the LIBRARY BILL OF RIGHTS states: "Libraries should challenge censorship in the fulfillment of their responsibility to provide information and enlightenment."

Article IV of the LIBRARY BILL OF RIGHTS states: "Libraries should cooperate with all persons and groups concerned with resisting abridgment of free expression and free access to ideas."

The American Library Association opposes any legislative or regulatory attempt to impose content restrictions on library resources, or to limit user access to information, as a condition of funding for publicly supported libraries and information services.

The First Amendment guarantee of freedom of expression is violated when the right to receive that expression is subject to arbitrary restrictions based on content.

Librarians and governing bodies should examine carefully any terms or conditions attached to library funding and should oppose attempts to limit through such conditions full and equal access to information because of content. This principles applies equally to private gifts or bequests and to public funds. In particular, librarians and governing bodies have an obligation to reject such restrictions when the effect of the restriction is to limit equal and equitable access to information.

Librarians and governing bodies should cooperate with all efforts to create a community consensus that publicly supported libraries require funding unfettered by restrictions. Such a consensus supports the library mission to provide the free and unrestricted exchange of information and ideas necessary to a functioning democracy.

The Association's historic position in this regard is stated clearly in a number of Association policies: 50.4 *Free Access to Information*, 50.9 *Financing of Libraries*, 51.2 *Equal Access to Library Service*, 51.3 *Intellectual Freedom*, 53 *Intellectual Freedom Policies*, 59.1 *Policy Objectives*, and 60 *Library Services for the Poor*.

Adopted by the ALA Council, June 30, 1993.

Appendix C:
Poverty Related Organizations

American Library Association (ALA) is a professional organization of mainly librarians and library administrators, but also friends and supporters. The ALA speaks for all types of libraries (public, school, academic, and professional) at the national level. The Public Information Office is a source of information, materials, and graphics. 50 East Huron Street, Chicago IL 60611; (312) 944-6780 or (800) 545-2433

American Public Welfare Association founded in 1930 is a nonprofit, bipartisan organization of individuals and agencies concerned with human services. The mission of APWA is to develop, promote, and implement public human service policies that improve the health and well-being of families, children, and adults. APWA educates members of Congress, the media, and the broader public on what is happening in the states concerning welfare, child welfare, health care reform, and other issues involving families and the elderly. 810 First Street NE, Suite 500, Washington DC 20002-4267; (202) 682-0100; fax: (202) 289-6555

Association of Community Organizations for Reform Now (ACORN) advocates the concept of a "majority constituency" (defined by ACORN as individuals of low to moderate income who are shut out of the power structure in this country). 1024 Elysian Fields Avenue, New Orleans LA 70117; (504) 943-0044; email: acorn@acorn.org

Center for Community Change assists community groups of urban and rural poor in making positive changes in their communities. Designs and delivers technical assistance, focuses attention on national issues dealing with human poverty, and works to make government responsive to the needs of the poor. 1000 Washington Avenue NW, Washington DC 20007; (202) 342-0519

Childwatch International is an international network for institutions and individuals involved in research for children with the aim of initiating and coordinating research and information projects on children's living conditions and the implementation of children's rights. Http://childhouse.uio.no/childwatch/index.html

Coalition on Human Needs (CHN) is an alliance of over 100 national organizations working together to promote public policies which address the needs of low-income and other vulnerable populations. The Coalition's members include civil rights, religious, labor and professional organizations and those concerned with the well-being of children, women, the elderly and people with disabilities. The Coalition also works with grassroots groups across the country that share an interest in the human needs agenda. 1000 Wisconsin Avenue NW, Washington DC 20007; (202) 342-0726; fax: 202-338-1856

Community Information Exchange is a national, nonprofit information service that provides community-based organizations and their partners with the information they need to successfully revitalize their communities. The Exchange was founded in 1983 to strengthen grassroots organizations, especially in poor neighborhoods and rural communities. The Exchange provides comprehensive information about strategies and resources for affordable housing, economic and community development, customizes this information for individualized inquiries, and offers technical assistance. 1029 Vermont Avenue NW, Suite 710, Washington DC 20005; (202) 628-2981; fax: 202-783-1485; e-mail: cie@comminfoexch.org Web: neighborlink.cc.duq.edu/cie/index.htm

Food First (Institute for Food and Development Policy) is a member supported, non-profit research and education-for-action center highlighting root causes and value-based solutions to hunger and poverty around the world, with a commitment to food as a human right. 398 60th Street, Oakland CA 94618; foodfirst@igc.apc.org http://www.netspace.org/hungerweb/FoodFirst/index.htm

Food Research and Action Center (FRAC) is a nonpartisan center seeking lasting solutions to hunger, malnutrition and poverty in America. By seeking improved federal food programs, greater economic opportunity for low-income people, and better protection of the rights of the impoverished, FRAC works to alleviate the hardships of hunger and poverty. 1875 Connecticut Avenue NW, Suite 540 Washington DC 20009; (202) 986-2200; fax: 202-986-2525; e-mail: hn0050@handsnet.org

Fourth World Movement/USA is a multinational group of volunteers working to bring about the full and free participation of the Fourth World in society. Organizes programs including street libraries, and literacy and computer projects 7600 Willow Hill Drive, Landover MD 20785 301-336-9489; e-mail: 4thworld@his.com

Habitat for Humanity is an Ecumenical Christian housing organization. It works in partnership with people in need throughout the world to build shelter that is sold to them at no profit through no-interest loans. 121 Habitat Street, Americus GA 31709-3498; (912) 924-6935

Housing Assistance (HAC) is a national nonprofit corporation founded in 1971 and dedicated to increasing the availability of decent housing for low-income people in rural areas. HAC works in every part of rural America but has an emphasis on high-need groups and regions: Indian country, the Mississippi Delta, farm-workers, the Southwest border colonies, and Appalachia. 1025 Vermont Avenue NW, Suite 606, Washington DC 20005; (202) 842-8600; fax: 202-347-3441; e-mail: HN0143@handsnet.org; Web: www.ruralhome.org

Institute for Children and Poverty (ICP) is the research and training division of Homes for the Homeless, which operates four American Family Inns in New York City. Each day these transitional housing facilities for homeless families provide education, job readiness training and support services to 540 families and 1,000 children. ICP works to provide innovative strategies to combat the impact of homelessness and urban poverty on the lives of children and their families. 36 Cooper Square, 1st Floor, New York NY 10003; (212) 529-5252; fax: 212-529-7698; e-mail: hn4061@handsnet.org; Web: www.opendoor.com/hf h/

Institute for Food and Development Policy empowers citizens to address the root causes of hunger, poverty, and environmental decline. Research and educational materials reveal how anti-democratic institutions and belief systems promote hunger and environmental deterioration. 398 60th Street, Oakland CA 94618; (510) 654-4400; fax: 510-654-4551; e-mail: foodfirst@igc.apc.org; Web: www.netscape.org/hungerweb/FoodFirst/index.htm

Jewish Fund for Justice is a Jewish philanthropic foundation dedicated to providing technical and financial assistance to grassroots community organizations combating the root causes of poverty on a non-sectarian basis. 260 Fifth Avenue, Suite 901, New York NY 10001; (212) 213-2113; fax: 212-213-2233.

Libraries for the Future is a national non-profit organization of public library advocates. LFF educates and activates current and potential library users to become advocates and to enhance the relationship between libraries and communities, particularly those with limited resources. The LFF program promotes community participation and universal access to literacy, lifelong learning and information, essential tools for democracy. 121 West 27th Street, Suite 1102, New York NY 10001; (212) 352-2330 or (800) 542-1918; fax: 212-352-2342; http://www/inch.com/~lff/lffhome.htm

National Association of Community Action Agencies consists of executive directors and board members of community action agencies and other agencies funded under the Community Services Block Grant. It represents community action agencies to promote a unified approach to solving the problems of poverty within the U.S.; and serves as an advocate of the poor at all levels of government. 1875 Connecticut Avenue NW, Suite 418, Washington DC 20009, (202) 265-7546

National Center for Children in Poverty seeks to identify and promote strategies that reduce the number of young children living in poverty in the United States, and that improve the life chances of the millions of children under six who are growing up poor. The Center projects concentrate on early childhood care and education; child and family health; family and community support; cross-cutting, multi-state policy analyses; demographic and evaluation research; and communications. http://cpmcnet.columbia.edu/dept/nccp/

National Coalition for the Homeless serves as a clearinghouse of information for social service and legal agencies, church organizations, private charities, community groups, and individuals interested in helping the homeless. 1612 K Street NW, Suite 1004, Washington DC 20006; (202) 775-1322; e-mail: nch@ari.net and http://www2.ari.net/home/poverty/

National Jobs for All Coalition is a network of concerned citizens and organizations committed to building a new movement for full employment. The Coalition includes individuals and organizations whose primary interest is in workers', women's, seniors' and children's rights, hunger and poverty prevention, civil rights and economic justice. The Coalition is committed to a sustainable peacetime economy and a democratic workplace that is supportive of families and communities, and that offers equality to groups traditionally disadvantaged in the workplace. 475 Riverside Drive, Suite 832, New York NY 10115; (212) 870-3449; e-mail: njfac@ncccusa.org

The National Low Income Housing Coalition (NLIHC) is the only national organization that is solely dedicated to ending America's housing crisis. Its mission is to ensure that housing is a human right for all people. 1012 Fourteenth Street NW, Suite 1200, Washington DC 20005; (202) 662-1530; fax: 202-393-1973; e-mail: info@nlihc.org; Web: www.handsnet.org/nlihc/

Oxfam America works in partnership with communities around the world to find long-term solutions to poverty and hunger. 26 West Street, Boston MA 02111-1206; (617) 482-1211; fax: 617-728-2594; e-mail: oxfamusa@igc.apc.org

The Poverty and Race Research Action Council is a non-partisan, not-for-profit organization convened by major civil rights, civil liberties and anti-poverty groups. The purpose is to link social science research to advocacy work in order to address problems at the intersection of race and poverty. 1711 Connecticut Avenue NW, #207, Washington DC 20009; (202) 387-9887; fax: 202-387-0764; e-mail: prrac@aol.com

Save the Children Federation was established in 1932 and operates as a voluntary, nonsectarian, nonprofit organization in the U.S. and throughout the world providing services for children and community self-help assistance. The mission of Save the Children is to make lasting, positive change in the lives of disadvantaged children. Efforts focus on four key issues: Education; Health; Economic Opportunities; and Humanitarian Response. 54 Wilton Road, P.O. Box 950, Westport CT 06881; (203) 221-4079; fax: 203-226-6709

Share Our Strength is the nation's leading anti-hunger organization that mobilizes industries and individuals to contribute their talents to fight hunger. By supporting food assistance, treating malnutrition and other consequences of hunger, and promoting economic independence among people in need, Share Our Strength meets immediate demands for food while investing in long-term solutions to hunger and poverty. 1511 K Street NW, Suite 940, Washington DC 20005; (202) 393-2925; fax: 202-347-5868; e-mail: SOS@charitiesusa.com Web: www.strength.org

Share the Wealth/United for a Fair Economy is an independent, non-partisan national organization based in Boston and begun in 1994. The mission of the group is to educate and activate citizens around issues of increasing economic inequality and insecurity. National Office: 37 Temple Place, 3rd floor, Boston MA 02111; (617) 423-2148; fax 617-423-0191; e-mail: Stw19@stw.org, web: www.stw.org/stw

Social Responsibilities Round Table Task Force on Homelessness, Hunger and Poverty takes an active role within the American Library Association in promoting libraries as places that can create social change. Contact SRRT through the American Library Association 50 East Huron Street, Chicago IL 60611; (312) 944-6780 or (800) 545-2433; fax: 312-944-2641; http://www.ala.org

Students Together Ending Poverty is a student-led, national organization working to strengthen the student role in the anti-poverty movement. STEP is committed to creating partnerships with the poor and homeless in order to eliminate the root causes of hunger, homelessness, and poverty. 8 Varney Street, Jamaica Plain MA 02130; (617) 5232-6924; e-mail: temery@igc.apc.org

Synergos Institute is a private, non-governmental, non-profit organization that works with voluntary organizations and other groups in supporting local communities to develop effective, sustainable solutions to poverty problems. 100 East 85th Street, New York NY 10029; (212) 517-4900

The Urban Justice Center, formerly the Legal Action Center for the Homeless is a regional advocacy organization which goes to soup kitchens to offer legal assistance to individuals who need help obtaining public benefits. The Center represents soup kitchen users in Fair Hearings before Administrative Judges when clients believe HRA has illegally terminated their benefits or denied them benefits. 27 W. 24th Street, Room 600, New York NY 10010; (212) 229-2080; fax: 212-229-2273

Welfare Mothers Voice is a news journal created by mothers on the edge. It gives a voice, information, and inspiration to mothers around the country who are suffering from poverty, isolation, and self-doubt. 2711 West Michigan Street, Milwaukee WI 53208; (414) 342-6662

Women in Community Service (WICS) founded in 1964, reduces the number of young women living in poverty by promoting self-reliance and economic independence. WICS actively addresses critical national issues surrounding employment, job training, welfare reform, poverty. and cultural diversity. 1900 N. Beauregard Street #103, Alexandria VA 22311; (703) 671-0500; fax: 703-671-4489; e-mail: WICSnatl@aol.com; Web: www.wics.org

Women Work! The National Network for Women's Employment is dedicated to empowering women from diverse backgrounds and assisting them to achieve economic self-sufficiency through job readiness, education, training, and employment. Women Work is committed to on-going, comprehensive public education to build awareness of the needs of women entering, re-entering, and/or training for the work force. 1625 K Street NW, Suite 300; Washington DC 20006; 202-467-6346; fax: 202-467-5366

World Hunger Year (WHY) is a national organization that promotes self-reliance, food security and economic justice through research and education for policymakers, the media and the general public and through collaboration with and support for the grassroots organizations. The mission is to work for just policies creating a more secure world and to support innovative programs creating sustainable livelihoods for all. 505 Eighth Avenue, 21st Floor, New York NY 10018-6582; (212) 629-8850; fax: 212-465-9274; e-mail: WHYRIA @aol.com; web: www.iglou.com/why

Bibliography

Agenda for Access: Public Access to Federal Information for Sustainability Through the Information Superhighway. A Report Prepared by the Bauman Foundation. Washington DC: Bauman Foundation, January 1995.

"ALA Membership and Council Approve Poor People's Services Policy Resolution." *Empowerment* 2, 1 (Summer 1990): 1–2.

Anderson, Frank Douglas. "What of the Information Poor?" *Library Review* 42, 1 (1993): 20–4

Behrman, Sara "Free and Equal Access to Library Services and Technology." In Sally Gardner Reed, ed., *Creating the Future: Essays on Librarianship* (Jefferson NC: McFarland, 1996): 244–251.

Berman, Sanford. "Fees, Fines and Poor People." *WLW Journal* 14, 3 (Spring 1991): 15–16.

Blake, Fay M. "Information and Poverty." In Jovian P. Lang, ed., *Unequal Access to Information Resources: Problems and Needs of the World's Information Poor* (Ann Arbor MI: Pierian Press, 1988): 12.

_____. "The Library's Commitment to the Public Sector." In E.J. Josey, ed., *Libraries, Coalitions, and the Public Good* New York: Neal-Schuman, 1987).

Blanke, Henry T. "Libraries and the Commercialization of Information: Towards a Critical Discourse of Librarianship." *Alternative Library Literature: A Biennial Anthology* (Jefferson NC: McFarland, 1992): 107–109. (Reprinted from *Progressive Librarian* 2 [Winter 1990–91]: 9–14.)

Brown, Eleanor Francis. *Library Service to the Disadvantaged.* Metuchen NJ: Scarecrow Press, 1971.

Bundy, Mary Leff, and Frederick J. Stielow, eds. *Activisim in American Librarianship, 1962–1973.* New York: Greenwood Press, 1987.

Buschman, John. "Asking the Right Questions about Information Technology." *American Libraries* 21, 11 (December 1990): 1026–1030.

_____. "Information Technology, Power Structures, and the Fate of Librarianship." In Sanford Berman and James P. Danky, eds., *Alternative Library Literature, 1992–1993: A Biennial Anthology* (Jefferson NC: McFarland, 1994). (Reprinted from *Progressive Librarian* 6/7 [Winter/Spring 1993]: 15–29.)

_____. "Myths of the Information Society: A Guide for Librarians." *Urban Academic Librarian* 9, No. 1 (Winter 1994): 4–17.

_____, ed. *Critical Approaches to Information Technology in Librarianship: Foundations and Applications.* Westport, Conn. : Greenwood Press, 1993.

_____, Mark Rosenzweig; and Elaine Harger. "The Clear Imperatives for Involvement: Librarians Must Address Social Issues." *American Libraries* 25, 6 (June 1994): 575–6.

Carlson, Pam. "Shining Stars: Public Library Services to Children in Shelters." *School Library Journal* 38 (July 1992): 18–22

_____, Sherry Des Enfants, Rachael W. Walker and Daryl L. Mark. "Libraries Can Serve Homeless Children." *Journal of Youth Services in Libraries* 7, 3 (Spring 1994): 255–71.

Chatman, Elfreda A. "Information, Mass Media Use and the Working Poor." *Library and Information Science Research* 7 (April 1985): 97–113.

_____. "Low Income and Leisure: Implications for Public Library Use." *Public Libraries* 24, 1 (Spring 1985): 34–36.

_____. "Opinion Leadership, Poverty, and Information Sharing." *RQ* 26 (Spring 1987): 341–53.

_____, and Pendleton, Victoria EM. "Knowledge Gap, Information-Seeking and the Poor." *Reference Librarian* 49/50, (???): 135–145.

Childers, Thomas. *The Information-Poor in America.* Metuchen NJ: Scarecrow Press, 1975.

Connor, Jean L. "The Ripple Effect: Patterns of Library Service to the Unserved as Seen from the State Level." In Lawrence L. Sherill, ed., *Library Service to the Unserved* (New York: Bowker, 1970): 61–70.

Curley, Arthur. "Obstacles to Information Access." In Jovian P. Lang, ed., *Unequal Access to Information Resources: Problems and Needs of the World's Information Poor* (Ann Arbor MI: Pierian Press, 1988): 1–8.

Davis, William P., John Swan and Sanford Berman. "Three Statements on Fees." In Sanford Berman and James P. Danky, eds., *Alternative Library Literature, 1990–1991: A Biennial Anthology.* (Jefferson NC: McFarland, 1992): 127–30. Statements made at the ALA Intellectual Freedom Committee Hearing on Fees, Chicago (Jan. 12, 1991)

Des Enfants, Sherry. "Libraries Can Serve Homeless Children: Project Horizons." *Journal of Youth Services in Libraries* 7 (Spring 1994): 259–64.

Diener, Richard A. V. "Informational Poverty and the Ascent of Ignorance." *Bulletin of the American Society for Information Science* 13 (Oct./Nov. 1986): 23, 36.

Dowd, Frances Smardo. "Homeless Children in Public Libraries: A National Survey of Large Systems." *Journal of Youth Services in Libraries* 9, 2 (Winter 1996): 155–164.

"Economic Barriers to Information Access: An Interpretation of the Library Bill of Rights." *Newsletter on Intellectual Freedom* (American Library Association), Sept. 1993: 137.

Fanelli, Vincent. *The Human Face of Poverty: A Chronicle of Urban America.* New York: Bootstrap Press, 1990.

_____, and Bruno Tardieu. *Passport to the New World of Technology...Computers.* Pierrelaye, France: ATD Fourth World, 1986.

Farrington, Polly-Alida. "Federal Documents on Homelessness." *Collection Building* 11, 3 (1991): 36–40.

Ferguson, Eleanor A., and Henry T. Drennan. "Services to the Unserved on the National Level: A Dialogue." In Lawrence L. Sherill, ed., *Library Service to the Unserved* (New York: Bowker, 1970): 55–60.

Foster, Andrew. *Public Library Outreach to the Disadvantaged*. Sheffield: University of Sheffield, Postgraduate School of Librarianship and Information Science, 1975.

Galman, Terry. "Food Pantries, Legal Aid, and the Third Word That Ends in -gry; Information and Referral with the Emphasis on *Information*." *Information and Referral* 18 (1996): 135–140.

Gaughan, Thomas M. "Rewarding Excellence, or Penalizing the Poor? (State Aid for Public Libraries in New Jersey)." *American Libraries* 19, 8 (Sept. 1988): 646.

Goldberg, Beverly. "Patron Charges Library Rules Preclude Service to the Poor." *American Libraries* 21, 11 (Dec. 1990): 1021–22.

Golightly, Cornelius L. "Examining Our Attitudes Towards the Unserved." In Lawrence L. Sherill, ed., *Library Service to the Unserved* (New York: Bowker, 1970): 11–24.

Gonzalez, Mario M., and Harriet Gottfried. "Library Services to the City's Homeless." *Bookmark* 46, 4 (Summer 1988): 229.

Haar, John M. "The Politics of Information: Libraries and Online Retrieval Systems." *Library Journal* 111, 2 (Feb. 1, 1986): 40–42.

Harris, Michael. "Public Libraries and the Decline of the Democratic Dogma." *Library Journal* 101 (Nov. 1, 1976): 2225–2230.

_____. "The Purpose of the American Public Library: A Revisionist Interpretation of History." *Library Journal* 98 (15 Sept. 1973): 2509–2514.

"Hennepin County Reaches Out to Low Income Families." *School Library Journal* 40, 10 (Oct. 1994): 14, 18.

Jones, Clara S. *Reflections on Library Service to the Disadvantaged*. Chicago: American Library Association, 1973.

Josey, E.J. "Libraries, Coalitions, and the Homeless," address delivered at the 1986 Annual Conference of the American Library Association, New York City, June 29, 1986.

_____. *Libraries, Coalitions, and the Public Good*. New York: Neal-Schuman, 1987.

Kangas, Sinikka, Timo Kuronen and Paivi Pekkarinen. "The Right to Information — The New Role of Libraries." *Libri* 45, 2 (June 1995): 123–29.

Kietel, Susan Lehman. "Libraries Need Help to Plug in Fast." *Viewpoints* (May 1, 1995): A24.

Kuehn, Jennifer J. "Homelessness: Interdisciplinary Collection Development Challenge." *Collection Building* 11, 1 (1991): 14–18.

Lakus, Priscilla, and Haymond, Stephanie. *The Library Reaches Out to Children with Special Needs: A Manual for Libraries and Librarians*. Tampa: Tampa-Hillsborough County Public Library System, 1993.

Lang, Jovian P., ed., *Unequal Access to Information Resources: Problems and Needs of the World's Information Poor* (Proceedings of the Congress for Librarians, Feb. 17, 1986). Ann Arbor MI: Pierian Press, 1988.

Lipsman, Claire K. *The Disadvantaged and Library Effectiveness*. Chicago: American Library Association, 1972.

Logan, Ann. "The Magic Bus Thrives on Diversity." *Colorado Libraries* 16 (Sept. 1990): 11–13.

MacCann, Donnarae. *Social Responsibility in Librarianship: Essays on Equality*. Jefferson NC: McFarland, 1989.

Malinconico, S. Michael. "Information's Brave New World." *Library Journal* 117, 8 (May 1, 1992): 36–40.

Martin, William J. *Library Services to the Disadvantaged*. London: Linnet Books and Clive Bingley, 1975.

Miller-Huey, Charles P. "'Brother, Can You Spare a Dime?' Homeless Patrons and Public Libraries." *Colorado Libraries* 20, 3 (Fall 1944): 30–34.

Minnesota Social Responsibilities Round Table. "Poor Peoples' Services." *Progressive Librarian* 1 (Summer 1990): 36.

Mosco, Vincent. *The Pay-Per-View Society: Computers and Communication in the Information Age.* Norwood NJ: Ablex, 1989.

Moses, Richard. "The Training of Librarians to Serve the Unserved: The 'High John' Project." In Lawrence L. Sherill, ed., *Library Service to the Unserved* (New York: Bowker, 1970): 71–78.

Murdoch, Faith T. "School Library Service in Disadvantaged Areas." In Lawrence L. Sherill, ed., *Library Service to the Unserved* (New York: Bowker, 1970): 45–51.

Myers, Glenda. "Robin Hood in Interlending: Charging the Information Rich to Help the Information Poor." *Interlending and Document Supply* 19 (Jan. 1991): 3–6.

Naidu, N. Guruswamy, ed. *Library Service for the Disadvantaged.* New Delhi: Ess Ess Publications, 1989.

Nassimbeni, Mary. "Libraries and Poverty." *South African Journal of Library and Information Science* 54, 1 (June 1986): 56–60.

Nauratil, Marcia J. *Public Libraries and Nontraditional Clienteles.* Westport CT: Greenwood Press, 1985.

"NYPL Takes Major Step to Aid Regional Economic Development." *Library Hotline* (Dec. 16, 1991): 1–2.

"Patron Charges Library Rules Preclude Service to the Poor." *American Libraries* 21, 11 (Dec. 1990): 1021.

"Petition on LC Headings." *Library Journal* 116, 9 (May 15, 1991): 24.

Pienaar, Rae E. "Survival Information: The Role of the Public Library in the Social and Cultural Development of Disadvantaged Communities." *IFLA Journal* 21 (1995): 15–18.

"Portland Reading Room Receives Funding." *Wilson Library Bulletin* 63, 5 (Jan. 1989): 15.

Pressman, Steven. "Poverty and Antipoverty Policy in 20th Century America." *Choice* 31 (May 1994): 1393–1405.

"Public Libraries Find Ways to Serve Urban Homeless." *American Libraries* 19, 4 (April 1988): 250–2.

Robinson, Charles. "The Public Library Vanishes." *Library Journal* 117, 5 (March 15, 1992): 51–54.

Schiller, Herbert I., and Anita Schiller. "Libraries, Public Access to Information, and Commerce." In Vincent Mosco and Janet Wasko, eds., *The Political Economy of Information* (Madison: University of Wisconsin Press, 1988).

Schuman, Patricia Glass. "'Information Justice.'" *Library Journal* 107, 11 (1 June 1982): 1060–66.

_____. "Social Goals vs. Public Interests: Players in the Information Arena Clash." *Publishers Weekly* 226, 21 (23 Nov. 1984): 56–58.

_____, ed. and comp. *Social Responsibilities and Libraries: A Library Journal/School Library Journal Selection.* New York: Bowker, 1976.

Schwartz, Edward. *NetActivisim: How Citizens Use the Internet.* Sebastopol CA: Songline Studios, Inc., 1996.

"Serving Homeless People: The Denver Public Library Protects Everyone's Right to Read." *Viewpoint* (Denver Public Library) 10, 3 (Fall 1994): 1–6.

Simmons, Randall C. "The Homeless in the Public Library: Implications for Access to Libraries." *RQ* 25 (Fall 1985): 110–120.

Spiller, Deborah J., and Michael Baker. "Library Service to Residents of Public Housing Developments: A Study and Commentary." *Public Libraries* 28, 6 (Nov./Dec. 1989): 358–61.

Swan, John C. "Rehumanizing Information: An Alternative Future." *Library Journal* 115, 14 (1 Sept. 1990): 178–82.

Sweetland, James II. "Information Poverty — Let Me Count the Ways." *Database* 16 (Aug. 1993): 8–10.

This Is How We Live: Listening to the Poorest Families. Landover, Md.: Fourth World Publications, 1995

"Towards a New World Information and Communication Order: A Symposium." In Sanford Berman and James P. Dankey, eds., *Alternative Library Literature, 1990–1991: A Biennial Anthology* (Jefferson NC: McFarland, 1992): 68–77. (Transcript of Progressive Librarians Guild–sponsored panel at 9th Annual Socialist Scholars Conference held in New York City on April 7, 1991.)

Vavrek, Bernard. "Access to Information: What a Difference Geography Makes." In Jovian P. Lang, ed., *Unequal Access to Information Resources: Problems and Needs of the World's Information Poor* (Ann Arbor MI: Pierian Press, 1988): 35–40.

Venturella, Karen M. "The Homeless and the Public Library." In Sanford Berman and James P. Dankey, eds., *Alternative Library Literature: A Biennial Anthology* (Jefferson NC: McFarland, 1992): 117–22. (Reprinted from *Progressive Librarian* 3 [Summer 1991]: 31–42.)

Voedisch, Ginni. "'Librarability — Access for All': A Conference and an Attitude." In Sanford Berman and James P. Danky, eds., *Alternative Library Literature, 1990–1991: A Biennial Anthology* (Jefferson NC: McFarland, 1992): 137. (Reprinted from *OCLC Micro* 6, 5 [Oct. 1990]: 32–39.)

Welbourne, James C., Jr. "Economics and the Black Urban Poor: The Grassroots Response." In *National Conference of the African American Libraries* (1st: 1992: Columbus OH). Chicago: Black Caucus of the American Library Association, 1993.

Werner, Judith. "Patterns of Library Service to the Unserved in Milwaukee." In Lawrence L. Sherill, ed., *Library Service to the Unserved* (New York: Bowker, 1970): 79–81.

Williams, Eva G. "Personnel and Materials for the Unserved: Unlocking the Doors." In Lawrence L. Sherill, ed., *Library Service to the Unserved* (New York: Bowker, 1970): 83–86.

Wilson, Alex. "The Information Rich and the Information Poor." *ASLIB Proceedings* 39, 1 (1987): 1–6.

Notes on Contributors

Khafre Abif was formerly the children's librarian at Southwest Branch, District of Columbia Public Library, Washington, D.C., and later, the Youth Services librarian at Montclair Public Library. Presently he is head of Children's Services at the Mount Vernon (NY) Public Library. He is coeditor of *In Our Own Voices: The Changing Face of Librarianship* (Scarecrow Press, 1996). He currently serves on ALA's International Relations Subcommittee on Africa, the ALA Social Responsiblities Round Table (SRRT), the Coretta Scott King Task Force, BCALA's E.J. Josey Scholarship Fund, and the BCALA International Relations Committee on Africa.

Sanford Berman is head of cataloging at Hennepin County Library in Minneapolis. He founded the ALA/SRRT Hunger, Homelessness and Poverty Taskforce and coedits *Alternative Library Literature: A Biennial Anthology.*

Yolanda Bonitch is the Manhattan Borough community specialist at New York Public Library. She is the recipient of the Sloan Public Service Award for Outstanding Public Service (1992) and the NYPL Bertha Franklin Feder Award for Outstanding Librarianship (1988). She earned a master's in education from Wagner College and her MLS from Pratt Institute. She authored *Libros en Español para los Pequeños* (1993) and "The Library Serves Homeless Children" (*Bookmark*, 1988).

John Buschman is a professor and librarian at Rider University where he is coordinator of collection development and department chair. His publications and papers on information technology have appeared in numerous professional journals. He is editor of *Critical Approaches to Information Technology in Librarianship* (Greenwood Press, 1993).

Pam Carlson is a children's specialist at the Westminster and Costa Mesa branches of the Orange County (Calif.) Public Library. She is grant director for the STAR project which established the library program at Orangewood Children's Home and is currently the librarian at the Orangewood Library. She is a former member of the California Young Reader Medal Committee,

Joshua Cohen, director for Outreach and Continuing Education at the Mid-Hudson Library System in Poughkeepsie, N.Y., is chair of the ALA Ethnic Materials Roundtable, a LAMA Publication Committee member, and a member of the New York State Commissioner's Advisory Committee on Adult Learning Services. He has published articles on focus groups and community assessment, and is a reviewer for *Library Journal* and *ARBA (American Reference Books Annual)*.

Denis Cretinon, originally from France, is a computer technician by training, and worked previously for five years with the Fourth World Movement in the Central African Republic. He is presently the program director of the New York City branch office of Fourth World Movement/USA.

Kathleen de la Peña McCook is a professor and director of the School of Library and Information Science at the University of South Florida. Currently she serves as the chair of the ALA Office for Literacy and Outreach Services Advisory Committee, as treasurer of the Florida Library Association, and as co-chair of the Tampa Bay Library Consortium Committee on Library Service to Migrant Farm Workers. She received her M.A. from the Graduate Library School, University of Chicago, and her Ph.D. from the University of Wisconsin School of Library and Information Studies.

Mildred Dotson, coordinator of Special Services at New York Public Library, is a four time recipient of the NYPL Special Performance Award (1988, 1990, 1994, 1996) as well as numerous other awards. Her professional activities include membership in ALA's Black Caucus, the Minority Concerns and Cultural Diversity Committee, the Public Library Association, the New York State Library Services and Construction Act Advisory Council (1986–1992), and the New York Literary Alliance. She also authored "Maintaining a Balance to Serve Learners," *Bookmark*, spring 1992.

Carl Egner has degrees in history and Asian studies, and worked for four years with the Fourth World Movement team in the Philippines. He is presently associate director at the national headquarters of Fourth World Movement/USA, in Landover, Maryland.

Sherry Lampman works as a consultant in developing community-based coalitions dedicated to such issues as literacy, the power of information, and economic security for families. From 1992 to 1996, she coordinated the Minnesota Alliance for Children's campaign to inform working families about the federal Earned Income Tax Credit and state Working Family Credit. As assistant director of Metronet, a multitype library system in the metropolitan area of Minneapolis and St. Paul, she coordinated the annual "Capitalizing on

Collaboration" library recognition process, the development of school-business partnerships focused on reading, and the cable television program "All About Kids!"

Kate Lippincott is a reference librarian at the Sarasota County Public Library in Sarasota, Florida. She was a research associate at the University of South Florida School of Library and Information Science, and a staff member in the Pullen Library at Georgia State University and also at the library at Birmingham-Southern College. Her recent publications include "Reaching Out to an Underserved Clientele: The Migrant Worker Family Project Committee" (1997) and "Twenty-five Years of Outreach" (1996).

Wizard Marks has worked as a school and city bus driver, and a reporter for neighborhood newspapers in Minneapolis. In 1973, she operated the first toy-lending library in the country for home day-care providers. As a board member of the Central Neighborhood Improvement Association, she became involved in the Hosmer Library project. She now directs the Chicago Lake Security Center, which is aimed at improving relations with the police and enhancing the Chicago Lake area.

Lillian Marrero is a bilingual librarian currently working as technology coordinator and trainer at the Ramonita G. de Rodriguez Computer Training Lab of the Free Library of Philadelphia (FLP). She has been working at the FLP for five years as an adult librarian providing services primarily to the Spanish speaking population. She is a member of the Association for Educational Communications and Technology, and REFORMA.

Sharon Morris, a librarian at the Denver Public Library, is responsible for outreach, programming, and video productions for the children's library. She has a B.A. in communications from Colorado State University and an M.L.S. from Emporia State University.

Elizabeth Segel taught children's literature for seventeen years at the University of Pittsburgh and publishes frequently on family literacy, emergent literacy, and children's literature. She is coauthor of *For Reading Out Loud: A Guide to Sharing Books with Children* (Dell). Dr. Segel and her colleague, Dr. Joan Friedberg, founded Beginning with Books.

Mary D. Teasley has been employed at the Newark Public Library in Community Library Services for over thirty years. She received her M.L.S. from Rutgers University and is currently Coordinator of Library Exhibitions and Programs.

Karen M. Venturella is head of multimedia resources at Montclair (N.J.) State University Library. Prior to becoming a librarian, she worked with the chronically mentally ill homeless in Philadelphia. She has her M.A. in Education

Psychology from Teachers College, Columbia University and her M.L.S. from the University of Pittsburgh.

Deloris Walker-Moses is the children's librarian and branch manager at Clinton Branch of the Newark Public Library. She pursued her studies at Essex County College, Kean College and Seton Hall University. She enjoys working with community outreach programs that are progressive, useful and valuable to the growth of all ages.

Samuel Weinstein has been with the Free Library of Philadelphia for twenty years, most of that time in the Acquisitions Department. For the past three years he has been involved in computer training, first for Free Library staff and then for the public as the project manager of the Rodriguez Branch Library Computer Training Lab. He is a member of the Association for Educational Communications and Technology.

Index